PENGUIN BOOKS

THE Q ANNUAL

Spike Milligan was born at Ahmednagar in India in 1919. He received his first education in a tent in the Hyderabad Sindh desert and graduated from there through a series of Roman Catholic schools in India and England to the Lewisham Polytechnic. Always something of a playboy, he then plunged into the world of Show Business, seduced by his first stage appearance, at the age of eight, in the nativity play of his Poona convent school. He began his career as a band musician, but has since become famous as a humorous scriptwriter and actor in both films and broadcasting. He was one of the main figures in and behind the infamous Goon Show. Among the films he has appeared in are: *Suspect, Invasion, Postman's Knock* and *Milligan at Large.* Spike Milligan has also published *The Little Potboiler, Silly Verse for Kids, Dustbin of Milligan, A Book of Bits, The Bed-Sitting Room* (a play), *The Bald Twit Lion, A Book of Milliganimals, Puckoon, Transports of Delight, Small Dreams of a Scorpion* and his war memoirs, *Adolf Hitler: My Part in His Downfall, 'Rommel?' 'Gunner Who?', Monty: His Part in My Victory* and *Mussolini: His Part in My Downfall.* Among his latest publications are *The Milligan Book of Records, Games, Cartoons and Commercials, Dip the Puppy, William McGonagall: The Truth at Last* (with Jack Hobbs), *The Spike Milligan Letters* (edited by Norma Farnes) and *Open Heart University.* Many of Spike Milligan's books are published in Penguin.

A rare photograph of
Hitler in the shower.

SPIKE MILLIGAN
THE

ANNUAL

PENGUIN BOOKS

Penguin Books Ltd, Harmondsworth, Middlesex, England
Penguin Books, 625 Madison Avenue, New York, New York 10022, U.S.A.
Penguin Books Australia Ltd, Ringwood, Victoria, Australia
Penguin Books Canada Ltd, 2801 John Street, Markham, Ontario, Canada L3R 1B4
Penguin Books (N.Z.) Ltd, 182-190 Wairau Road, Auckland 10, New Zealand

First published in Great Britain by Michael Joseph,
in association with M&J Hobbs, 1979
Published in Penguin Books 1980

The author and publishers gratefully acknowledge the BBC
for permission to reproduce most of the illustrations in
this book, and also Popperfoto for those on pages 68, 82,
88 and 119; the Press Association for the picture on
page 36; and Syndication International for the one on
page 19. The publishers also wish to thank the author
for allowing them to reproduce the illustrations on
pages 103, 107, 126 and 128.

Made and printed in Great Britain by Butler & Tanner,
Frome and London

Dedication

To Her Majesty The Queen, or Mrs. Thatcher, or whoever's turn it is to hand out the OBEs, I dedicate this volume, in return for which I would like to be considered for a fitting for a knighthood, bearing in mind that

KENNY LYNCH

PETER SELLERS

HARRY SECOMBE

JIMMY YOUNG

have all received Birthday Honours, and as I am touching 93, could you consider some kind of meritorious medal I might get on your next birthday – GROVEL, GROVEL, BOW, SCRAPE, WINK, NUDGE, NUDGE, SAY NO MORE. You will not ever get a more honest and direct request for a knighthood than this.

After all I'm whiter than Kenny Lynch
     lighter than Harry Secombe
        and taller than Peter Sellers – and I don't wear a wig.

Your humble servant

Spike Milligan

Pip, Squeak and Wilfred are dead and therefore will not be appearing in this book

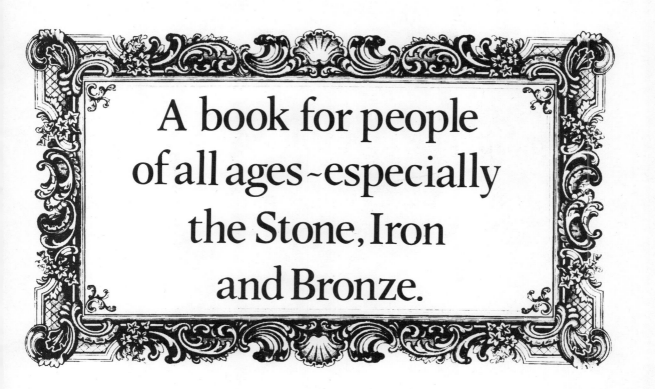

A book for people
of all ages ~ especially
the Stone, Iron
and Bronze.

ATTENBOROUGH'S TRAVELS

AS PER ATTENBOROUGH'S 'TRIBAL EYE' SHOW, A SERIES OF BEAUTIFULLY PRESENTED TRIBAL GODS, IDOLS, ETC. BACKGROUND MUSIC OF AFRICAN DRUMS AND CHANTING.

SOUND MIXES THROUGH TO SOUND OF STREET BARREL-ORGAN PLAYING 'LAMBETH WALK'.

THE GOD IMAGES NOW TURN TO A BOTTLE OF LIGHT ALE REVOLVING, BEAUTIFULLY PRESENTED AND LIT.

EMPTY PINT GLASS WITH FROTH DOWN THE SIDES.

ASHTRAY FULL OF DOG-ENDS.

THEN AN OPEN NEWSPAPER WITH FISH HEADS AND A FEW CHIPS.

Caption: THE TRIBAL HIGH.

A SERIES OF DOCUMENTARIES ON PRIMITIVE PEOPLE.

THIS WEEK – THE COCK A KNEES.

A SLUM REDEVELOPMENT AREA – PAN ACROSS DEVASTATION TO SPIKE AS ATTENBOROUGH.

SPIKE WEARS OVER-LARGE, KNEE-LENGTH SHORTS, OVERSIZE BROWN BOOTS, SOCKS HANGING DOWN, AND A KHAKI SHORT-SLEEVED SHIRT.

SPIKE WALKS ACROSS DERELICT AREA, CAMERA FOLLOWS.

Spike   During the past weeks we saw the natives of the Septic River tribes from New Guinea, and in Melanesia, the Aku Aku Islanders with their mystic belief in Thor Heyerdahl, the great God of sinking rafts. This week we visit a lost white tribe which no black man has ever seen, the Cock a nees.

HE COMES TO A LETTER-BOX.

They have many varied beliefs, some strange and some incomprehensible. For instance this. They believe if you feed a message into the mouth of this red Iron God, then a uniformed devil will come, rip open the stomach of the God, take the contents away, and lose them. That is why the written language has ceased to exist. Instead . . .

HE MOVES TO AN ADJACENT PILE OF RUBBISH, ON TOP OF WHICH IS AN OLD TV SET.

Spike   . . . they use this strange box

The opening speaker at the Annual Dinner of the 'Look Like Rasputin' Society being stricken with haemorrhoids.

to communicate (*switches on*).

RICHARD BAKER APPEARS ON SCREEN, SAYS 'GOOD EVENING. HERE IS THE 9 'OCLOCK NEWS.'

NEW LOCATION: Ruined derelict building with stairs going up.

Spike   They speak a strange patois; they call these the Apples. They believe if you ascend the apples, you come to a chamber where a white goddess awaits them.

CUT TO 1930 GROTTY WORKING-CLASS BEDROOM. BRASS DOUBLE BED. OLD DEAR OF 50 SMOKING A FAG, HAIR IN CURLERS, IS TAKING OFF OLD-FASHIONED CORSETS. SHE WEARS BLOOMERS AND A LONG VEST.

Spike   These early films taken by a white health inspector missionary show a male Cock a nee, going through an elaborate courtship display.

THIS FILM IS IN SEPIA, UNDERCRANKED, WITH THE SOUND OF CONGO DRUMS IN BACKGROUND.

OLD MAN STARTS TO PEEL OFF HIS CLOTHES, REVEALING LONG UNDERPANTS, SOCKS WITH HOLES IN, VERY VERY TATTY AND PATCHED.

Spike   He strips away his drab exterior plumage to reveal a surprising delicate underlayer. To arouse the female further, he dons what are called Winceyette pyjamas, and by drawing his fingernails across his body he induces a pre-sexual trance.

MAN PUTS ON PYJAMAS AND STARTS TO SCRATCH HIMSELF. HE PICKS THE PO FROM UNDER THE BED AND EXITS.

Spike   The ceremonial vessel called the Gezzunda is taken out and purified for the night.

THE OLD DEAR LIGHTS THE GAS FIRE WITH A MATCH.

Spike   The female is aroused by this, ignites a mysterious Captain Webb firestick, obviously a tribute to some early settler, and lights a sacred fire which bears these hieroglyphics.

CLOSE-UP ON GAS FIRE: 'NORTH THAMES GAS BOARD.'

Spike   The wrath of this God can only be appeased by incessantly feeding it votive offerings. She now performs a secret rite known only to the women of the tribe.

SEE THE WOMAN PUTTING MONEY INTO THE METER. WOMAN NOW CREEPS TO MAN'S TROUSERS, FEELS IN HIS POCKETS AND REMOVES MONEY, WHICH SHE STUFFS IN HER VEST OR KNICKERS.

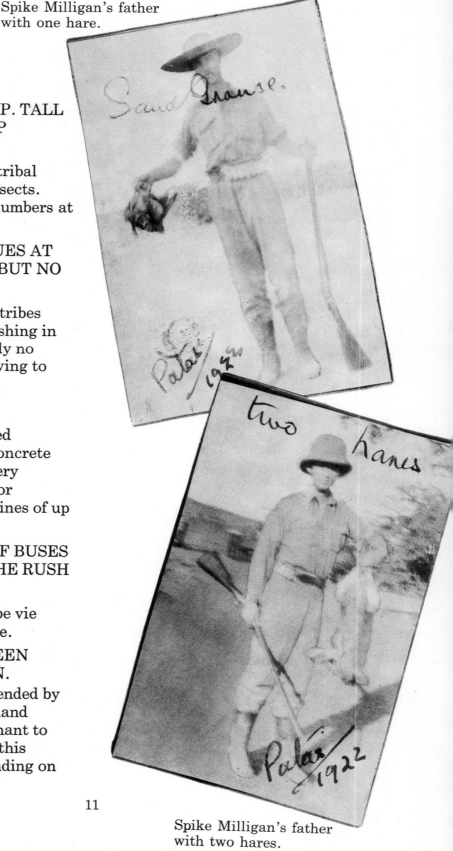

Spike Milligan's father
with one hare.

CUT TO A BUS STOP.

SEE ONLY THE BUS STOP. TALL WITH LOTS OF BUS STOP NUMBER-PLATES ON.

Spike This is a powerful tribal totem and attracts various sects. They gather here in large numbers at dawn and sunset.

FILM OF MASSIVE QUEUES AT RUSH-HOUR BUS STOP, BUT NO BLOODY BUSES.

Spike At these hours the tribes become visibly agitated, rushing in all directions with seemingly no purpose in life. They are trying to catch one of these.

FILM OF A BUS.

Spike Huge red landlocked monsters which roam the concrete jungle. They only appear very rarely, and when they do, for protection, they appear in lines of up to twenty.

FILM OF A LONG LINE OF BUSES CLOSE TOGETHER, IN THE RUSH HOUR.

Spike Members of the tribe vie with each other to catch one.

TERRIBLE FIGHT BETWEEN PASSENGERS TO GET ON.

Spike The monsters are tended by a black tribe from another land called Pa ke sta nes, who chant to the crowd – I'll try and get this right – (*Pakistani*) 'No standing on

Spike Milligan's father
with two hares.

Spike Milligan brings news
from the Underworld that the
tubes and the lavatories are
running.

top', 'Pass along the bus, please',
and 'There's another one behind.'

CUT TO SPIKE STANDING IN
SHOPPING PRECINCT.

Spike This is where the tribe grow
their food, and hunt.

SPIKE WALKS INTO FISH AND
CHIP SHOP. SEVERAL PEOPLE
BEING SERVED, PUTTING SALT
AND VINEGAR ON, ETC. BEHIND
COUNTER IS A FRYER.

SPIKE IS STANDING NEXT TO AN
ASSISTANT COCKNEY FISH
FRYER.

Spike Can you ask the hunter
what he is doing?

2nd Fryer Yes, I'll try. (*Goes into
Cockney*) 'Ere Eric, this is going to
kill yer.

1st Fryer Go on, then, tell us, I
can't wait.

2nd Fryer This geezer wants to
know what yer doing?

1st Fryer Wot am I doin? I'm
frying bleedin' fish, ain't I?

2nd Fryer He says he's frying
bleeding fish, isn't he?

1st Fryer Tell 'im it's a right
bleedin' job an all, you got soppy
hapoths comin' in here half Brahms
and Liszt asking for a piece of rock,
two skate, tanner's worth of chips,
and they give yer a twenty pound
note for it. It makes you want to
bloody spit.

2nd Fryer He says the gods are angry.

THE FISH FRYER TAKES OUT A
BASKET OF FISH, PLACES ONE
IN A BIT OF NEWSPAPER. (THE
SUN, PAGE 3 NUDE).

Spike The hunter has caught the
fish in one of these boiling rock pools
and places it on native matting, which
they believe has come from the Sun.

SUNDAY MORNING

LINE OF CARS IN SUBURBAN
STREET ALL BEING WASHED AND
POLISHED BY HUSBANDS. ALL
HAVE TRANSISTOR RADIOS ON
DIFFERENT NETWORKS.

SPIKE WALKS IN.

Spike This is the day of the Sun,
when the males of the tribe offer
homage to the family idol, which is
revered and worshipped above all
else (*he turns to a polishing lunatic*).

Spike Mo toe kar?

Man Yer, motor car. Three point
four jag . . . twin overhead cams . . .
with a compression ratio of 86.4 to 1
and a snip at 380 quid.

Spike 'A snip at 380 quid.' Now
that would only mean something to a
member of the AA tribe, who are
looked down upon by the great RAC
tribe who live in another world.

WE CUT TO SPIKE OUTSIDE THE
STREET LEVEL OF AN
UNDERGROUND STATION.

Spike These are the famous
disappearing holes, people go down
here and are never seen again.
But with the help of a tribal
elder, I decided to investigate

12

CUT TO TICKET INSPECTOR AT TOP OF DESCENDING ESCALATOR.

Inspector   Yer, many years ago, when I was a nipper, they told a story of a nuvver tribe called, er, Micks, who come from across the waters with strange artifacts.

HE INDICATES A TABLE ON WHICH ARE LAID OUT A PICK-AXE AND A SHOVEL, GUINNESS BOTTLES, NAVVY'S BOOTS, THE *CATHOLIC HERALD* AND A BETTING SLIP.

SPIKE LOVINGLY FONDLES THEM. THE PICK-AXE:

Spike   How did this instrument evolve? Why does it strike terror into the hearts of all men who see it? We carried out an experiment on the Mick sub-tribe.

FILM OF FIVE IRISH LABOURERS PLAYING CARDS ON A BUILDING SITE.

SPIKE APPROACHES WITH THE PICK-AXE COVERED WITH A CLOTH. HE PULLS IT OFF AND THE WORKMEN SET OFF SCREAMING.

RETURN TO SUBWAY. SPIKE PICKS UP A BETTING SLIP.

Spike   This finely worked piece of paper bears the legend Ladbrokes. Mill Reef, two bob each way. Shall we ever know what reef that was?

Was it the reef that Thor Heyerdahl foundered on in his attempt to prove that a raft made of Guinness Bottles and boiled potatoes was how Saint Patrick discovered Golders Green? All these are mysteries yet to be answered.

BOTTOM OF ESCALATOR LOOKING UP AT CROWDS DESCENDING.

Spike   These are the Kom mu ta tribe. Such is their fear of the outer world, they seek refuge in these ancient tunnels. They push forward blindly, hurling themselves into these tombs . . .

FILM OF JAPANESE UNDERGROUND RUSH HOUR, CROSS CUT WITH ENGLAND.

Spike   . . . which are then sealed, and driven away to remote burial grounds with strange sounding names like Upminster, Cockfosters, East Finchley and Ealing Common.

CUT TO COUNTRYSIDE. A SIGN: 'TIP NO RUBBISH'.

Tip No Rubbish, another strange place-name.

SPIKE IS STANDING BY THE SIGN. AT BOTTOM OF SIGN IS A LITTER BASKET. IT'S EMPTY.

Spike   The Cock a nee erects these wayside shrines, such is their reverence for them. They make a

14

point of never putting anything in them.

PULL BACK TO SHOW THE AREA COVERED IN RUBBISH, TINS, BOTTLES, ETC.

CUT TO A POND WITH BEDSTEAD, FIREPLACE, BICYCLE FRAME IN THE MIDDLE.

Spike But particularly moving is the sacrifice of the mattress, the bedstead and the bicycle frame to the ever-hungry God of the village pond.

SPIKE ON TOP OF STEPS LEADING DOWN TO A GENTS' LAVATORY.

This is the holy of holies, the sacred temple where no woman may enter.

PAN TO SIGN SAYING 'GENTS'.

CAMERA FOLLOWS SPIKE DOWNSTAIRS, TO THE ATTENDANT IN THE ROOM READING A PAPER.

Spike This is Bert Noble, a handmaiden of the temple. He worships the sacred pools called Littlewoods. The Cock a nees come here to seek relief in these cells of meditation.

FILM ROW OF WCs AS SPIKE WALKS DOWN THEM.

Spike Let us listen to them at their devotions.

SOUND OF STRAINING. PAPER. GRUNTS. SEATS DROPPING.

Spike If you listen carefully you will hear the music of the water God. A fitting end to this remarkable people, the Cock a nees. One wonders what will happen to them when civilization catches up with them.

MAN RUSHES DOWN THE STAIRS.

Man Out the bleedin' way.

BURGLARS

Spike Knock, knock, knock
(*On an invisible door*)

A man is heard saying Come, come, coming down the hall.

He appears and says Walk, walk, walk . . .

HE IS DRESSED LIKE A FRENCH WAITER. GOES THROUGH MOTIONS OF UNLOCKING AND UNBOLTING.

Clinck clinch, click whoosh, open.

Spike Good evening, we have reason to believe that you are the man standing in the hall.

Man Yes . . . but he's out. Can I help.

Spike My partner and I are devout Jehovah burglars.

Man But I'm Jewish.

Spike We'll come to that later. We are here because the police are persecuting us for our beliefs.

THE TWO MEN HAVE NOW ENTERED THE HALL.

Man What are your beliefs?

Spike We believe that you have some very valuable silverware and krugerands.

Man (*to camera*) Good heavens, that's absolutely true.

Spike (*to camera*) Well, we only believe in the absolutely true, brother.

THE SECOND MAN IS NOW PUTTING AWAY SILVER CANDELABRA. HE IS TAKING IT FROM A CAREFULLY LAID DISPLAY ON ABOUT A SIX-FOOT-LONG SHELF OF SILVERWARE, ABOVE WHICH IS THE SIGN: 'VERY VALUABLE SILVERWARE – SHOULD BE KEPT IN A SAFE.'

Man What are you doing.

Spike You.

Man But you're taking that very valuable silverware that should be kept in a safe (*reads notice from the wall*). It's mine.

THE SACK INTO WHICH THE MAN IS PLACING THE SILVERWARE HAS NO BOTTOM – EVERYTHING KEEPS FALLING THROUGH.

Spike Did you hear that, brother?

Spike Milligan heavily disguised as Batman compressing something below the waist. Robin is hiding in his mask.

We have a disbeliever amongst us. Let me convert you.

THE MAN KNEELS DOWN.

Spike   Close your eyes and say after me: Oh my bleedin' 'ead.

MAN BEHIND HIM THUDS HIM WITH A SOFT COSH.

Man (*toppling over*)   Oh my bleedin' 'ead. 'Ere comes the ground.

CUT TO POLICE STATION. THERE'S A PIMPLY POLICE CADET WITH CHEQUERED CONSTABLE'S HELMET. SPIKE RUSHES IN FROM PREVIOUS SET, AND PUTS ON POLICEMAN'S HELMET. ON A FLAT BEHIND HIM THERE'S A MAP OF LONDON ON THE WALL AND A LITTLE LIGHT BLEEPING IN IT.

Cadet   Sergeant, there's just been a distinct thud on the head at 356A Hagley Road, Birmingham.

Spike (*looking at camera*)   This is a job for the police.

STARTS TO DIAL 999.

BACK TO HALLWAY. LUMP-ON-HEAD MAN TRUSSED UP IN CHAIR. HE NOW HAS A LUMP ON HIS HEAD, A RED LUMP, WHICH IS HELD ON BY A PIECE OF ELASTIC UNDER THE CHIN. THE REMAINING JEHOVAH BURGLAR IS OPENING A LARGE IRON SAFE DOOR IN THE WALL. HE OPERATES THE DIAL. THE

DOOR OPENS, REVEALING THE POLICEMAN, THE CADET AND THE DOG. THEY STEP THROUGH INTO THE ROOM.

Spike   Good evening, we have traced a lump on the head to this address.

THE DOG GOES TO BURGLAR.

Sgt   Heel, Fang.

Dog   'Heel, Fang,' he says.

Sgt   I'm afraid I'll have to arrest your wrists.

Burglar   In connection with what?

Sgt   In connection with your arms.

Burglar   You can't arrest me – I'm a distant cousin of the Queen.

SPIKE IMMEDIATELY CONTORTS HIMSELF ON THE FLOOR.

Spike   You've put me in a very difficult position.

Dog   Lend him a quid till he's straight.

Sgt   Good boy, Fang.

Cadet   Sarge, there's someone coming down the stairs.

Dog   Quick, under the table.

THEY ALL RUSH UNDER THE TABLE.

AN OLD MAN APPEARS ON STAIR LANDING, HOLDING A PO AND A POKER.

Old man   Oh, I'm sorry. My wife

The Queen and Family watching the Q Series on TV.

thought she heard policemen down here. Oh dear, I'll be better soon.

THERE'S A TERRIFIC EXPLOSION FROM WHERE HE WAS JUST STANDING. A LOT OF CLOTHING. SEVERAL SETS OF CLOCKWORK CHATTERING TEETH DESCEND ON THE SET. EVERYBODY WILL IGNORE THEM.
THEY COME OUT FROM UNDERNEATH THE TABLE WITH HANDCUFFS, HUGE HANDCUFFS, AND PUT THE HANDCUFFS ON THE BURGLAR. THEY FALL TO THE GROUND. DURING ALL OF THIS THE DOG IS BARKING. THEY PUT HANDCUFFS ON AGAIN AND THEY CRASH TO THE FLOOR AGAIN.

Sgt   So, trying to escape, eh? I arrest you for being Houdini.

Burglar   Let me clear up the mystery.

AND THE SGT AND THE BURGLAR WALK UP AND DOWN LIKE MATES.

Burglar   The reason why these handcuffs fall off is because I am extremely thin due to malnutrition brought on by VAT.

19

Chinese Cabaret

Voiceover And now . . . testing, testing, testing . . . 'allo (blowing into mike), the Riviera Catford is proud to present from merry Hong Kong the cabaret sensation of the year 1929. And here he is, China's very own Grotty Thing.

Spike Molly, now pull out the swords.

AS GIRL PULLS OUT SWORDS WE HEAR BIG BASIE BAND ACCOMPANIMENT.

SPIKE COMES OUT OF THE MAGIC CABINET COVERED WITH BITS OF ELASTOPLAST ON FACE. HE WEARS WHITE TUNIC WHICH IS RIPPED BY SWORDS AND WE SEE BLOODSTAINS.

Spike (*as Chinaman*) Gleat to ble black in old cluntly. Funny thing happened to me on way to thleatre. I go chish and fip shop. I slay, Any chips keft? and he slay: Yeah. And I slay, Serve you broody light for flying so many . . . Ha ha ha . . . Ah well, can't win 'em all. Now for next tlick, Is there thin climinal in audience?

Thin Criminal This could be my lucky night.

THIN CRIMINAL GOES INTO THE BOX AND DISAPPEARS. SPIKE RIPS OFF CHINESE MAKE-UP.

Spike Ladies and gentlemen, I'm not really Grotty Thing. I'm a policeman and I've finally trapped this fiend. This could mean promotion for me. I know you're in there. Come out, because I'm coming in.

HE DIVES INTO THE BOX. WE SEE CURTAINS INSIDE. HE PLUNGES THROUGH. CUT TO REVERSE OF CURTAINS. THE SCENE IS AN ICE FLOE WITH A HOLE CUT IN THE MIDDLE. AN ESKIMO FISHING. ESKIMO IS LAUGHING AND POINTING INTO THE HOLE IN THE ICE. SNOW IS FALLING. IMMEDIATE SOUND OF BLIZZARD.

Spike Ladies and gentlemen, I've appeared in many police sketches in my time and this has been one of them. Goodnight all. (*To Eskimo*) Did he really go down there?

HOW TO POSE FOR FAME:

Take 6 in. Nail – drive through knee from right to left. Grab protruding ends in hands – lift upwards until leg is clear of ground. Hold pose until photographer appears. Fame will follow, as will blood poisoning.

The First Irishman in Space

CLOSE-UP OF GUINNESS BOTTLES, GIRLIE MAGAZINES, TINS AND RUBBISH. PULL BACK TO SEE DERELICT RUINED BUILDING AREA. FOCUS ON ONE RUINED BUILDING.

Caption: A HOUSE OF ILL REPUTE IN IRELAND.

Zoom into sign saying: DUBLIN LABOUR EXCHANGE. FOR OPENING TIMES SEE 'WHAT'S ON IN LIVERPOOL'.
WE SEE TWO RAGGED-ASSED IRISHMEN. ONE OF THEM IS PUSHING A WHEELBARROW, THE OTHER SITS IN IT.

Caption: AN IRISH TAXI.

ONE MAN EMPTIES THE OTHER ON TO THE PAVEMENT.

Caption: 'DAT'LL BE TREE SHILLINGS.'

CUT TO INSIDE LABOUR EXCHANGE. EVERYBODY INSIDE IS IN RAGS, UNSHAVEN, BLACK RINGS UNDER THE EYES WITH HEAVY SILENT FILM MAKE-UP. THERE ARE SUSPICIOUS LOOKS WHEN SPIKE ENTERS. LIKE SOMEONE ENTERING A SALOON IN A WESTERN CLICHE. SPIKE GOES UP TO COUNTER, AND SPEAKS TO A RAGGED MAN (THE CLERK) WITH BLACK HAIR PARTED IN THE MIDDLE.

Caption: ANY FEAR OF WORK?

CUT TO CLERK SPEAKING:

Caption: 'YES, THERE'S A JOB GOING.'

IMMEDIATELY THE TEN RAGGED MEN IN THE LABOUR EXCHANGE LEAP THROUGH WINDOWS, HURL THEMSELVES OUT OF THE DOOR. TWO OF THEM HAVE HEART ATTACKS AND COLLAPSE.

CLERK IS SPEAKING.

Caption: 'DEY NEEDS A DRIVER FOR DER FIRST OIRISH ROCKET TO DER MOON.'

CUT TO SPIKE SPEAKING.

Caption: 'BEDAD AND BEGORRAH, DAT'S JUST THE JOB I'VE BEEN WAITIN FOR.'

CUT TO DERELICT STRETCH OF GROUND. RUINED BUILDINGS ADJACENT.

Caption: DE OIRISH SPACE CENTRE, FISH SHAMBLE STREET, DUBLIN.

CUT TO TIN WORKMEN'S HUT. IN THE MIDDLE IS A SMALL COAL BRAZIER, AND FACING IN TOWARDS IT FROM EACH SIDE THERE IS A SEAT.

Caption: DE OIRISH LUNAR ROCKET GUINNESS TREE.

ENTER SPIKE WITH ANOTHER RAGGED IDIOT, WEARING WHITE BOILER SUITS WITH A LARGE SHAMROCK INSIGNIA ON THE LEFT BREAST. THEY HAVE WORLD WAR I GAS-MASKS ON THEIR CHESTS AND ARE WEARING WELLINGTON BOOTS AND YELLOW SAFETY HELMETS WITH THE WORD WIMPEY ON THE FRONT. THEY WALK IN AND SIT DOWN.

Caption: DE ASTR O'NAUTS.

PRIEST COMES IN AND BLESSES THE ASTRONAUTS.

Caption: DAVE ALLEN.

THEY APPEAR TO TIE THICK ROPES AROUND THEIR WAISTS.

WE PAN DOWN TO SEE THAT THE HUT IS RESTING ON BLACK BOXES WITH TNT IN WHITE.

WE CUT TO AN IDIOT SITTING ON AN ORANGE BOX HOLDING THE END OF A FUSE. HE HOLDS A BOX OF MATCHES, GRINNING AT CAMERA. HE IS ON A LONG HALTER TIED TO A TREE.

Caption: MISSION CONTROL, SLIGO.

HE STRIKES THE MATCH AND APPLIES IT TO THE FUSE, AND SHOUTS.

Caption: 'FAITH STAND BY FOR BLAST-OFF!'

WE FOLLOW THE FUSE AS IT BURNS. A LONG SHOT OF THE HUT WITH TWO DUMMIES NOW IN PLACE OF THE ORIGINAL ACTORS.

Caption: THE COUNTDOWN STARTS.

SERIES OF FIGURES COME UP ALTERNATELY.

Caption: 'TEN
　　　　SEVEN
　　　　THREE
　　　　NINE
　　　　SIX
　　　　WHAT'S NEXT, MICK?'

CUT TO LONG SHOT OF WHOLE HUT EXPLODING.

Caption: 'WE HAVE LIFT-OFF.'

CUT TO INTERIOR OF DUBLIN LABOUR EXCHANGE.

UNEMPLOYED MEN ALL AROUND. THIS TIME THERE IS A BIG BREWER'S CARTHORSE. IN COME OUR HEROES, SMOKE-BLACKENED. THE CLERK SPEAKS.

Caption: 'Now what?'

SPIKE SPEAKS

Caption: 'We bin fired.'

CLERK SPEAKS

Caption: 'Don't worry, dere's annuder rocket leavin' at half past tree.'

SPIKE SPEAKS

Caption: 'Wot's der time now.'

CLERK ANSWERS.

Caption: 'Er – it's exactly that.'

CLERK HOLDS WATCH IN FRONT OF SPIKE.

SPIKE SPEAKS

Caption: 'So it is.'

CLERK SPEAKS

Caption: 'But dis time youse got to take der horse.'

SPIKE REACTS VIOLENTLY

Caption: 'Why?'

CLERK SPEAKS

Caption: 'Because he's unemployed.'

FILM OF ALBERT MEMORIAL.

Caption: IRISH SPACE ROCKET II

CUT TO A LARGE, GRILLED, FRONTED LUGGAGE LIFT. ENTER THE ASTRONAUTS, WHO LEAD HORSE INTO LIFT.

CUT TO FILM OF PHONE-BOX, ONE BLUE-SUITED IDIOT STANDING OUTSIDE AND ANOTHER ONE IS INSIDE. THE DOOR IS OPEN. HE'S PUTTING TWO PENCE IN.

Caption: 'Mission Control, Kilburn.'

MAN IN PHONE-BOX IS LOOKING AT A LARGE CHEAP ALARM-CLOCK. HE IS HOLDING WHITE HANDKERCHIEF AS IF STARTING A RACE. HE SPEAKS.

Caption: 'All Systems Go.'

SPIKE HAS PHONE TO HIS EAR AND IS PRESSING LIFT BUTTON.

LIFT STARTS UP. THEY LOOK TERRIFIED. THEY EXPECT AN EXPLOSION. IT DOESN'T HAPPEN.

SPIKE SPEAKS.

Caption: 'It's a bird. Break open der space food.'

SECOND MAN IS POURING GUINNESS.

Caption: 'Live from Guinness II.'

SPIKE SPEAKS TO THE HORSE.

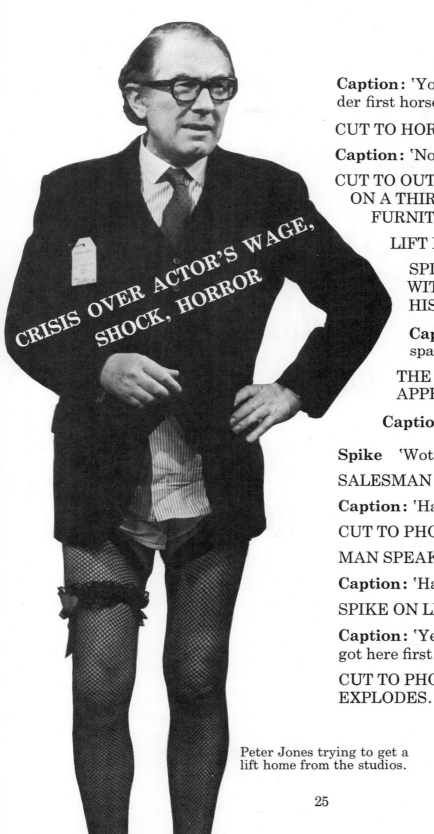

CRISIS OVER ACTOR'S WAGE, SHOCK, HORROR

Caption: 'You, sir, are going ter be der first horse on der moon.'

CUT TO HORSE, FACE ON

Caption: 'Nothing on it.'

CUT TO OUTSIDE OF A LIFT ON A THIRD FLOOR FURNITURE DEPT.

LIFT DOOR OPENS.

SPIKE COMES OUT WITH A ROPE ROUND HIS WAIST.

Caption: 'First Irish space walk.'

THE SALESMAN APPROACHES.

Caption: 'Can I help you, sir?'

Spike 'Wot place is dis?'

SALESMAN

Caption: 'Harrods.'

CUT TO PHONE-BOX.

MAN SPEAKS.

Caption: 'Has yez got to der moon?'

SPIKE ON LIFT PHONE SPEAKS

Caption: 'Yes. Bad news. Harrods got here first.'

CUT TO PHONE-BOX, WHICH EXPLODES.

Peter Jones trying to get a lift home from the studios.

Why are two Union Jacks like Margaret Thatcher's knickers?

I don't know, why are two Union Jacks like Margaret Thatcher's knickers?

Because no power on earth can pull them down!

Marlborough Country

WE SEE IN THE DISTANCE IN SLOW MOTION A MAGNIFICENT HORSE AND COWBOY IN FULL MARLBORO' COUNTRY GEAR.

WE CUT TO A HERD OF CATTLE THUNDERING IN THE DISTANCE, ALSO IN SLOW MOTION.

A GREAT SLOW MOVING ROMANTIC ORCHESTRAL THEME.

THEN VOICEOVER: A DEEP AMERICAN VOICE:

Voiceover   Come to Duke of Marlborough country . . . where the flavour is.

IMMEDIATE CLOSE-UP OF COWBOY ON HORSE COUGHING HIS LUNGS OUT.

CLOSE-UP OF HORSE COUGHING LUNGS OUT.

CLOSE-UPS OF HERD OF CATTLE COUGHING LUNGS OUT.

LONG SHOT OF ALL THREE AGAINST THE SUNSET. MUSIC OUT, AND JUST THE SOUND OF COUGHING.

CUT TO HOSPITAL WARD. SPIKE IN OXYGEN TENT.

Spike   Since I changed to Honson and Bedges Low Tar, I've felt much better. Until then (*cough*) I only had eight days to live. Now I've been given twelve. (*coughs*).

Voiceover   Honson and Bedges . . . the cigarette that gives you just that little bit more.

WE SEE SPIKE COLLAPSE.

It's the Governor of the Bank of England, he's left a suicide note.

Wot's it say?

I promise to pay the bearer one pound on demand.

The Idiot Scout Troop

FILM CLIP FROM WARTIME MOVIE OF RALPH READER DRESSED AS A NAVAL OFFICER. HE SINGS AND DANCES 'WE'RE RIDING ALONG ON THE CREST OF A WAVE'.

CUT TO EXTERIOR OF GROTTY SCOUTS' HUT.

FROM INSIDE WE HEAR THE SOUNDS OF IDIOT LAUGHTER.

Interviewer (*on long walk round hut*) These happy sounds of idiot laughter hammering and banging are in fact the happy sounds of idiot laughter hammering and banging. They are England's only idiot scout troop. They all joined when they were seven and have failed every knot-tying test, woodcraft, and fire-lighting test, but such is their enthusiasm Lord Baden Powell didn't have the heart to tell them. Strangely, this year they have shown remarkable powers of recovery. For instance they can dress themselves. Let's go inside and talk to their senior sixer.

INSIDE THE HUT IS CHAOS. A LARGE CENTRE TABLE. AROUND IT ARE FIFTY-YEAR-OLD SCOUTS, WITH HUGE SCOUT HATS DOWN OVER THEIR EYES, HUGE SCOUT SHIRTS AND VOLUMINOUS KHAKI SHORTS. THEY ALL HAVE HUGE FALSE STOMACHS AND KAISER WILHELM MOUSTACHES. THEY ARE ALL LAUGHING LIKE IDIOTS. IN THE BACKGROUND THERE ARE THREE OR FOUR HANGING BY THE NECK.

Senior Sixer I'm Lord Baden Powell.

Int What's going on back there?

Senior Sixer That's the knot-tying class.

Int Who are the four hanging from the beams?

Senior Sixer They're learning to untie knots . . . of course, we do lose a lot.

CONSTANT HAMMERING AND BANGING GOING ON, WITH

28

Spike Milligan as the BBC weatherman testing for rain. The Hitler moustache was a ruse.

IDIOT LAUGHTER IN VARIOUS PARTS OF HUT.

IN ONE CORNER AN AGED SCOUT IS PUTTING ON A 78 RECORD OF RALPH READER'S RECORDING OF 'RIDING ALONG ON THE CREST OF A WAVE'.

RECORD IS IMMEDIATELY WHIPPED OFF AND SMASHED WITH A MALLET. ANOTHER BERK PUTS ANOTHER IDENTICAL VERSION ON, WHICH IN TURN IS TAKEN OFF AND SMASHED. IDIOT LAUGHTER EVERY TIME THEY DO IT.

NEXT TO THIS THERE ARE TWO IDIOTS WITH JIGSAW SET, AND THEY ARE HAMMERING THE WRONG PIECES IN.

Senior Sixer These are our prize students. They've solved the problem of putting jigsaw puzzles together with the wrong bits.

A FEW CLOSE-UPS OF PIECES BEING HAMMERED IN. ALL THE FINGERS OF THE LEFT HANDS ARE BANDAGED AND EVERY TIME THEY HAMMER THEY HIT THEIR FINGERS AS WELL. CLOSE-UPS OF BITING PIECES OFF THE JIGSAW PUZZLE PIECES. ANOTHER BLOKE HAS A PAIR OF PLIERS WITH WHICH HE CLIPS PIECES OFF.

Senior Sixer Linda Lovelace has asked to see me.

THE MALLETS THEY USE ARE OVERSIZE – THE ONES THEY USE TO HAMMER DOWN PAVING STONES.

CUT TO A TABLE WITH ABOUT TEN CUPS FULL OF TEA ON IT. ONE IDIOT IS POURING ALL OVER THE PLACE, THERE IS TEA SLOPPING EVERYWHERE. ONE IDIOT DRINKS FROM THE CUP, PASSES IT TO A THIRD IDIOT WHO SMASHES IT.

Int What's this here?

Senior Sixer Those are the cups we drink tea out of.

Int Well, why is he smashing them?

Senior Sixer They don't know how to wash up.

THE SMASHED CUPS ARE PASSED ALONG TO A FOURTH IDIOT, WHO IS ASSEMBLING THEM TOGETHER WITH BITS OF SCOTCH TAPE AND MASKING TAPE, BUILDING THEM INTO THE MOST GROTESQUE SHAPES.

Senior Sixer And Leonard 'ere mends 'em.

Int Why?

Senior Sixer We can't afford new ones.

Int But they're all leaking.

Senior Sixer We'll soon lick that . . .

WE CUT TO A VERY BEAUTIFUL
FILM OF NUDE WOMEN.

Senior Sixer   This is the sex
education class.

PULL BACK TO SEE THESE
AGED IDIOTS ALL WITH A
BOXING GLOVE ON THEIR RIGHT
HAND, ALL LOOKING AND
ARGGHING AND ORRGING
LASCIVIOUSLY.

Senior Sixer   They're all over fifty
'ere, and the day can't be far off
when they realize that the ones that
go backwards in the dances are girl
guides.

WE COME TO AN IDIOT WITH A
PIANO KEYBOARD WITH ONLY
ONE NOTE ON IT. ALL THE
OTHERS HAVE BEEN REMOVED,
AND ALL THAT'S THERE IS
MIDDLE C. THE IDIOT IS
HITTING IT AND OH OH OH-ING
ALONG WITH IT.

Spike Milligan's brother and
sister-in-law – Sydney, Australia.

Newsdesk

Spike Good evening. Welcome to Q6, the show that keeps the rain off.

ADJACENT TO SPIKE IS A NEWSDESK. ON IT IS A PARCEL. HE WALKS TO DESK, SHOWS HE IS WEARING NO TROUSERS.

Spike It's from Princess Anne. (*Opens box and reads card*) 'Spike darling, I always send you one of these when you do a TV series, wear it for me.'

HE TAKES AWFUL FALSE NOSE FROM BOX, PUTS IT ON.

Spike Isn't Royalty wonderful? Thanks, Anne. And Mark, don't take it too bad, you've always got the horses.

Spike Milligan cunningly disguised as someone else.

HEIGHT SKETCH

A FRONT DOOR. NEXT TO IT A MAN IS STRANGLING A MAN WHILE A SECOND MAN HITS HIM ON THE HEAD. MAN BEING STRANGLED WEARS A PRINCESS ANNE GIFT NOSE.

Policeman Mrs Terrible?

Woman Yes.

Policeman Wife of Ivan Terrible, the one who works on the oil rigs in dangerous shark-infested waters during raging force 9 gales?

Woman Yes . . . is it bad news?

Policeman Yes, very bad . . . my wife's run off with a burglar (*Cries*).

Woman There, there, I'll give you some good news . . . Princess Anne will be 25 on the 15th August.

Policeman (*smiles*) I do believe I feel better already. (*Looks at men strangling each other*). I wonder if these men know Princess Anne will be 25 on the 15th August.
Do you know these people?

Woman The one that's being strangled is my lodger. I don't know the other two.

POLICEMAN BLOWS WHISTLE. THE TWO ASSAILANTS IMMEDIATELY SHOUT.

Assailant Look out . . . he's got a whistle.

THEY RUN TO CORNER AND TAKE OUT THEIR OWN

33

WHISTLES. THERE FOLLOWS A WHISTLE BATTLE, PEEPING ROUND CORNER AND BLOWING. CUT BACK TO POLICEMAN HIDING IN DOORWAY BLOWING HIS WHISTLE BACK. SEVERAL MORE POLICE WHISTLES ARE HEARD APPROACHING. THEY ALL TAKE UP WHISTLE-BLOWING POSITIONS.

Assailant Don't blow any more, copper, we give up.

Policeman Throw out your whistles and come out with yer hands over your ears.

THE ASSAILANTS THROW THEIR WHISTLES IN, AND COME OUT WITH HANDS OVER EARS.

Policeman (*to camera*) But I had made a grave mistake. These two men were in fact plainclothes policemen, and they were apprehending a plainclothes criminal.

ORIGINAL MAN WHO WAS BEING STRANGLED SPEAKS.

Man (*to camera*) Yes, you see, I am six feet tall, but I was in a five feet nine zone.

Policeman Therefore I cautioned him so (*turns to man*): Sir, you are exceeding the legal height by inches three.

Man I want to see a lawyer.

POLICEMAN HANDS HIM A TELESCOPE THAT HE IMMEDIATELY CLASPS TO HIS EYE.

Policeman There's one in that window up there.

CUT TO A COURTROOM. THE WHOLE COURT IS BUILT CRUSHED TOGETHER. THE JUDGE'S BOX IS ALMOST ON TOP OF THE WITNESS BOX. IN THE WITNESS BOX IS THE ACCUSED, SUSPENDED BY A KIRBY WIRE THAT CAN PULL HIM UP, IN THE UPRIGHT POSITION. HE WEARS A LONG RAINCOAT THAT WILL BE ABOUT TWENTY FEET LONG. THE DESIRED EFFECT IS THAT WHEN HE IS HOISTED 20 FEET, THE COAT WILL UNFOLD, THE BOTTOM HALF STILL ON THE FLOOR OF THE WITNESS BOX. THE ACCUSED WEARS A PRINCESS ANNE GIFT NOSE. THE DEFENDING COUNSEL ALSO WEARS A PRINCESS ANNE GIFT NOSE.

Defence M'lud, my client admits being six foot in a five foot nine area.

ALL THE CAST GO INTO OVERACTED MUMBLES OF SURPRISE.

Judge (*bangs desk with mallet that breaks in two*) Silence, I will not have overacting in my court. (*Looks at camera and smiles.*)

Defence I appeal to camera three,

my client claims mitigating circumstances. He was drunk, and lost control of his height.

Judge Did you get a doctor's report?

Defence No, we got a builder's estimate.

Judge Why?

Defence It was cheaper, and can a lady with a wooden leg change a pound note?

Judge Yes.

Defence No.

Judge Why not?

Defence She's only got half a nicker.

COLOSSAL BURST OF CANNED LAUGHTER.

Judge Silence, I will not have canned laughter in my court. (*Returns to judge character.*) Now, will you explain why your client is wearing that ridiculous nose?

Defence He's in love with Princess Anne, your Hon.

Judge Is that why you're wearing one?

Defence Yes, M'lud.

Judge Why is yours bigger?

Defence I've known her longer.

Judge Ronald Biggs, of no fixed trousers, you are accused of being

Princess Margaret & Roddy Llewellyn at the time the Q Series was being made.

illegally tall in Lewisham. How do you plead?

Accused I plead like this.

IMMEDIATELY SNOW STARTS TO FALL. NEXT TO HIM IN THE BOX, A POVERTY-STRICKEN WOMAN WITH BLACK HEADSHAWL HOLDING A BUNDLE STANDS UP AND CRIES.

MUSIC: THEME FROM TCHAIKOVSKY'S 'ROMEO AND JULIET'.

Accused (*goes into terrible overacting sadness*) I've got a wife and ten kids and she's in the club again. I was at Dunkirk, I had it shot off. . . .

Judge I'm sorry, your plea has failed to get the maximum number of points. Ronald Biggs, inside leg 32, I sentence you to be hung by the neck until you are inside leg sixty-seven. Do you plead guilty or not guilty?

HERE HE IS HAULED UP TWENTY FEET SHOUTING.

Accused I am innocent, innocent!

Defence My client has gone to a higher court.

The Plague of Liberaces

THE PHONE ON THE WALL BEHIND SPIKE RINGS. HE TURNS AND FACES IT.

Spike   Hello, Rodent HQ at your service.

SPIKE TAKES THE PHONE OFF HOOK.

Spike   Hello.

SPLIT SCREEN SHOWS THE CALLER, A MIDDLE-AGED WOMAN.

Woman   Hello, this is Queen Elizabeth the Second.

Spike   Yes, your Majesty?

Woman   I've got vermin in me throne room.

Spike   Royal Vermin? This is the big time! I'll send a man over right away tomorrow morning.

OPEN UP PICTURE OF WOMAN ON PHONE. SHE IS STANDING IN THE HALL. SHE HANGS UP.

Woman (*to camera*)   I shouldn't have told him I was Queen Elizabeth II, it's a lie, but it's the only way to get service these days. Ask any Queen.

SPIKE AND ASSISTANT WALK IN.

Spike   Hello, Mrs Queen, where are the Royal vermin?

CUT TO FRONT ROOM. SITTING AROUND IN CHAIRS, MIMING PIANO-PLAYING, ARE SIX LIBERACES. THEY ALL WEAR LIBERACE WIGS, AND THEY HAVE A FALSE, WHITE-TOOTHED LIBERACE GRIN FIXED ON THEIR MOUTHS, SUPERHUGE EXAGGERATED GRINS, ALL TEETH AND INSINCERITY. THEY ALL WEAR BLACK TROUSERS AND GLITTER JACKETS, BLUE FRILLY EVENING DRESS SHIRTS, VELVET BOW-TIES. THEY ALL KEEP MURMURING 'It's really wunnerful, ladies an' gentlemen.' INTO THE ROOM COME THE WOMAN AND THE OPERATORS.

Woman   Well?

Spike   They're not mice . . . Can I be honest with you?

Woman   Let me have it.

Spike   Later, madame, first the vermin. I'm sorry to tell you that you're suffering from a plague of Liberaces.

Woman   Liberaces, I'd rather have rats!

SPIKE WALKS TO A WHITE GRAND PIANO. IN THE TOP OF THE LID IS A MAN-SIZE HOLE.

Spike   This is where they're getting in.

Woman   Wot causes Liberaces?

Spike   A hatred of music. Have you got any glitter clothes spangles?

Woman   Yes, I have several pairs of spangled Gary Glitter-knickers.

Spike   Well, that's what attracts them. (*To camera*)   There's only one cure for Liberaces . . . the Jewish piano.

CUT TO ROOM WITH THE LIBERACES. SOUND OF A CASH-TILL BELL.

CUT TO SPIKE IN A GARDEN. THERE'S A MAN-SIZE MOUSETRAP, AND INSIDE IT IS A CASH TILL. THROUGH THE BARS SPIKE KEEPS RINGING UP A SALE. THE LIBERACES ALL RUN IN, THE TRAP CLOSES.

BACK TO ROOM – ALONG THE SKIRTING BOARD, THROUGH

HOLES, HANDS WITH PISTOLS APPEAR AND FIRE.

Spike   And do you know, lady, you've got assassins in your skirting?

Woman   Would you like a happy ending?

Spike   Yes.

Woman   Upstairs on the bed then.

Spike   What's wrong with the hall?

Spike Milligan sings his evening dress suit to sleep.

PHOTO SHOP

A PHOTOGRAPHY SHOP. VERY STARK SET. BEHIND COUNTER STAND A SALESMAN (SPIKE) AND A BOSOMY GIRL.

Caption BBC ECONOMY SET WITH ECONOMY ACTORS. ENTER A CUSTOMER.

Caption SIR PARTINGTON-KNICKS, CHIEF INSPECTOR OF POLICE.

Spike Yes, sir?

Customer Er, I'm getting married in the morning –

Spike Ding dong the bells are gonna chime then –

Customer I'd like to hire a photographer.

GIRL FAINTS.

Spike I'll just take down the address of the church. (*He prepares pencil and paper.*)

Customer She's fainted!

Spike (*ignores girl, writes down*) Sesssssss . . . Fainted . . . That's a funny address for a church.

Customer No, the girl's fainted.

Spike Oh dear, so she has . . . Good job the ground broke her fall. Now, the church?

Customer St Martins Le Grand. Look, aren't you going to help her?

Spike Business before pleasure, sir. If you like you can unfasten her blouse, massage under . . .

SPIKE STARTS TO GET A FLASH CAMERA READY.

. . . her heart.

THE CUSTOMER STARTS TO DO SO, REVEALS GIRL HAS A VERY SKIMPY BRA ON BIG BOSOM.

Customer She's not responding to it!!!.

Spike Well, she's unconscious. Try the kiss of life.

THE CUSTOMER NOW HAS HIS HAND UNDER THE GIRL'S BOOB AND IS KISSING HER.
SPIKE TAKES FLASH PHOTO.

Spike Ah, that'll look nice in 'The News of the World'. Chief of Police ravishes unconscious girl with big boobs.

Customer How did you know I was Chief of Police?

Spike I saw the caption come up in the beginning.

Customer Look, give me that camera . . . I'll give you £20.

Spike That's bribery.

Customer £50.

Spike That's a deal.

CUSTOMER FEVERISH

Trafalgar – A direct hit.

...VES MONEY TO SPIKE AND
RUNS OUT WITH CAMERA.
GIRL GETS UP.
Spike There must
be an easier way
to sell cameras.

Another direct hit.

Pakistani Daleks

Caption THE ORDINARY WORKING CLASS HOME OF A MIXED PAKISTANI-CHRISTIAN MARRIAGE. IT IS FRIDAY. WIFE IS LAYING THE TABLE. SHE'S ABOUT 40-ISH. MIXED ALONG THE HOUSE ARE TOUCHES OF ISLAMIC INFLUENCES. A BRASS GOD ON THE MANTELPIECE. A PARROT IN CAGE ON STAND. A STUFFED DOG BY FIREPLACE. A GRANNY IS DOZING BY THE FIRE. THE WIFE HUMS A TUNE. THE DOOR TO THE ROOM EXPLODES, AND THROUGH IT COMES A DALEK WITH TURBAN ON AND A FOLDED UMBRELLA HANGING FROM HIS SIDE. WOMAN DOESN'T TURN ROUND.

Dalek (*Pakistani accent*) Hel-oh, Dar-ling, I-am-back.

Woman You are late tonight.

Dalek The tubes were full of comm-u-ters.

Woman How did you get on then?

Dalek I ext-er-min-ated them.

Woman Oh, no wonder you're tired.

Dalek Yes, ex-ter-min-ating is hard work.

Woman Never mind, I've got a nice cup of curried tea for you. How's Mr Banerjee?

Dalek Not ver-y well.

Woman Why?

Dalek I ex-ter-min-ated him too.

DOG IN THE GRATE BARKS 'WOOF, WOOF, WOOF'. DALEK POINTS EXTERMINATOR AT HIM. SHOOTS. DOG EXPLODES

Dalek Put him in the Cur-ry.

SECOND DOOR TO ROOM EXPLODES, A TWO-THIRD SIZE DALEK WITH SCHOOL CAP ON COMES IN. IT AIMS AT A VASE ON MANTELPIECE. IT EXPLODES.

Woman Johnny, have you finished your homework?

Boy Dalek Yes. I de-str-o-yed it.

HE POINTS EXTERMINATOR AT
SLEEPING GRANNY.

Woman   You've exterminated
granny!

Dalek   Put her in the Cur-ry.

Parrot   Hello, sailor . . . Hello . . .

SHOOTS PARROT IN CASE.

Dalek   Put him in the Cur-ry.

Woman (*to camera*)   Now you know
what's wrong with this country.

ANOTHER EXPLOSION AS TV
SET OR SOME OBJECT BEHIND
HER EXPLODES. AS WE FADE
OUT THE TWO DALEKS DESTROY
VARIOUS OBJECTS: CLOCK ON
MANTELPIECE, VASES,
LAMPSTAND.

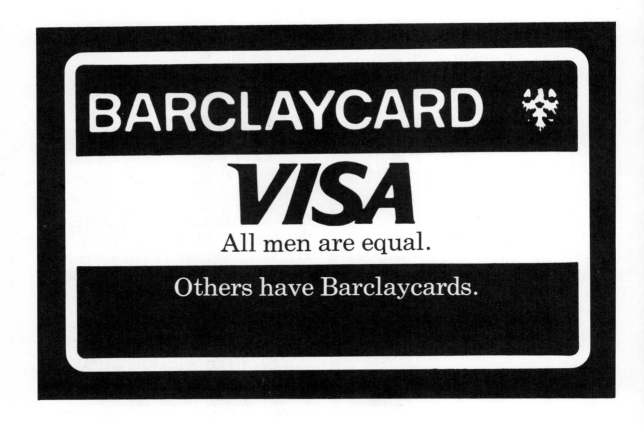

WARDROBE

A LONDON STREET. PARKED
CAR. WARDEN GOES TO STICK
FINE ON WINDSCREEN, IT
HASN'T GOT ONE. HIS ARMS
DISAPPEAR THROUGH. HE SEES
A CLOTHES CUPBOARD ON PRAM
WHEELS PARKED BY THE KERB.
HE HEARS THE SOUND OF A
ROW BETWEEN MAN AND
WOMAN, DISHES BEING
THROWN. HE LOOKS THROUGH
KEY HOLE. POLICEMAN
APPEARS.

P.C. 'Ello 'ello? Wot have we got
'ere? A Peeping Tom?

Warden My name's Dick.

P.C. Worse. A Peeping Dick.

Warden I am innocent.

ENTER WOMAN WITH SHORT
WHITE TOWEL, MID-THIGH.

Woman Don't believe him, this
man is a voyeur, and he spies on me.

P.C. When?

Woman Thurdays at ten,
Wednesdays and Mondays
two-thirty.

P.C. Which part of you has he
spied on?

Woman Mainly my knees.

P.C. Well, madame, if he spies any
higher ring us and make a
complaint; if he gets any lower, ring
him and make a complaint.

Woman Thank you.

P.C. Now, madame, would you like
to accompany me behind a bush and
bring my police career to a close?

EXIT PURSUED BY A BEAR.
HORNS, ALARMS. OUT OF THE
CUPBOARD STEPS A SAILOR,
HIS HATBAND SAYS GLC FLATS.

Warden Hello, sailor.

Sailor None of that, I am not a
Hello sailor but a sailor serving on
Her Majesty's GLC Flats . . . and
when you insult me you insult the
Queen.

Warden Well, you can't park that
mahogany and spruce wardrobe
there, and when you insult me you
insult Mrs Flo Terrible of Ongar.

Sailor But it's taxed and licensed.

It's an antique, road tested by Arthur Negus.

Warden Antique? Then you'll need a ten-year MOT test.

Sailor MOT? How do you spell that?

Warden (*looks at notebook*) MINISTRY OF TRANSPORT. Pronounced MOT.

WOMAN'S VOICE FROM INSIDE WARDROBE.

Woman (*slight echo*) I regret it, you'll regret it, it was your bloody mother-in-law, look at the bleedin' lino!

SOUNDS OF CROCKERY BREAKING.

Warden What you got in there?

Sailor It's my divorce. (*Whistles hornpipe and does dance.*)

Warden A divorce? In a wardrobe.

Sailor Yes, she got custody of the children, I got custody of the wardrobe. I pay her £2,000 a week alimony.

Warden Cor, stone a crow!

Sailor Well, she's the Queen's cousin. (*Whistles hornpipe and dances.*) £2,000 is the rate for Queens' cousins, it would have been more if it had been the Queen's sister: five grand. And if *I'd* have divorced the Queen . . .

AT MENTION OF THE WORD QUEEN, WARDEN CROSSES HIMSELF.

. . . I'd be walking round with the arse out of me trousers.

Warden (*to camera*) I don't consider her much of a Queen, marrying a man with the arse out of his trousers.

Sailor (*to camera*) This man has obviously mistaken me for Prince Philip. (*Whistles hornpipe and dances.*)

Warden (*crosses himself*) How *do* you find the money?

Sailor Very nice (*grins*).

Policeman (*rushes in, stands still, blows whistle*) Has a black vicar with a dwarf nude nun found strangled under bed murder been committed here?

Warden No.

Policeman I'll try round the corner. (*Runs off blowing whistle.*)

Warden That man has obviously mistaken me for a black vicar with a strangled dwarf nude nun under my bed.

CUT TO POLICE STATION. TWO BENIGN SERGEANTS IN CHARGE ROOM. ON WALL IS A CHART WITH HEADING 'CONSTABLE BRIGHTOLS MURDERS'.

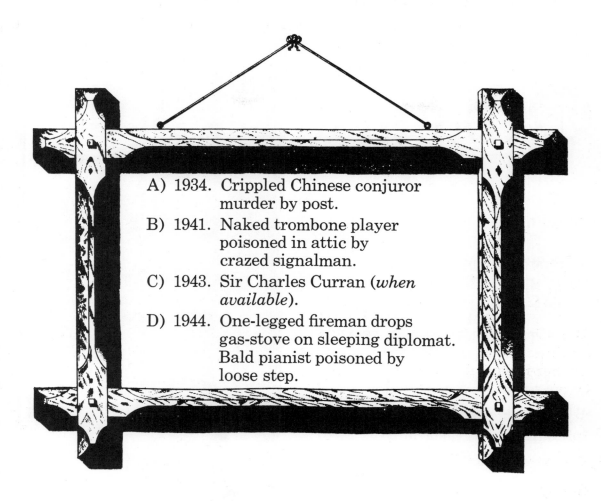

A) 1934. Crippled Chinese conjuror murder by post.

B) 1941. Naked trombone player poisoned in attic by crazed signalman.

C) 1943. Sir Charles Curran (*when available*).

D) 1944. One-legged fireman drops gas-stove on sleeping diplomat. Bald pianist poisoned by loose step.

THE POLICEMAN COMES RUNNING IN CRYING. SOBS IN CORNER.

Sergeant   What's up, Bill?

Policeman   It's no good. I've got the . . . (*reads off list from board*). But the one I haven't got is black vicar with a dwarf nude under bed murder. Then I've got the . . . I got the set . . .

RETURN TO WARDROBE SCENE.

Woman (*voice inside*)   Johnnnnn . . . John. Hurry.

Warden   Hear that, she's got John Hurry in there with her.

Sailor   Another man? I'll see. (*Whistles hornpipe and goes in.*)

Sailor   There was another man. Thank God he wasn't in. I'll never play that piano again.

Warden   This is no way for a Queen's cousin to treat a GLC sailor.

HE OPENS CUPBOARD. INSIDE IS AN ORDINARY MAN'S SLEEVELESS VEST ON A WIRE HANGER.

Ordained

QUEUE OF PEOPLE AT A BUS
STOP. ENTER SHERLOCK
HOLMES AND DOCTOR WATSON
WITH BUS STOP SIGN. THEY
WALK TO FRONT OF QUEUE AND
PUT SIGN ON PAVEMENT.
HOLMES CARRYING LARGE
HANDHELD MAGNIFYING GLASS,
BUT NO GLASS IN IT.

Spike (*Holmes*)   Elementary.

Watson   Brilliant.

SOUND OF BUS APPROACHING.
A SKELETON WITH BUS
CONDUCTOR'S HAT ON IS PULLED
BY IN THE GUTTER.

Sherlock (*to camera*)   I have reason
to believe there is only a skeleton
service tonight.

Watson   Brilliant.

SUDDENLY AN ARCHBISHOP OF
CANTERBURY IN FULL KIT
RUSHES UP WITH HIS CROOK.
POINTS PISTOL AT COMMUTER.

Archbishop (*in harsh Brooklyn
voice*)   OK, you dirty rat, you . . .
Hands together, kneel down.

Spike Milligan trying to have
it away with Katie Boyle
under very difficult
circumstances. (Note Queen
in left-hand corner of photo.)

COMMUTER KNEELS DOWN.

Archbishop   OK, now, blue eyes. Et tuam, dedicadum, it servitor Christium, Semper fideli. Amen.

HE RUNS OUT. VICTIM SCREAMS AND CRASHES TO GROUND HOLDING HIS THROAT AND GROANING. SHERLOCK PRODUCES GIANT HANDHELD MAGNIFYING GLASS, PASSES IT OVER VICTIM.

Sherlock   This man is lying on the ground, holding his throat, groaning and overacting.

Watson   Brilliant.

Sherlock   He has black greasy hair.

Watson   Brilliantine.

SHERLOCK TAKES MAN'S HANDS FROM THROAT, OPENS UP HIS OVERCOAT TO REVEAL HIS NECK. THE MAN IS WEARING A CLERICAL COLLAR AND BLACK FRONT.

Sherlock   Good God . . . he's been . . . ordained.

MUSIC: CRASHING ORGAN CHORDS, BACH'S D MINOR TOCCATA AND FUGUE.

Watson   Ordained, you say? Who do you suspect?

Sherlock   It looks like a typical Archbishop of Canterbury job to me.

Victim   I'm Jewish.

Sherlock   Now the bad news . . . You're now a Christian.

Victim   Ohhh, mein life . . .

Sherlock   We must get him to a de-ordination clinic.

Victim (*change of character to a parson*)   Dearly beloved, we are gathered here today . . .

Sherlock   There, there . . . it's starting to take!

ALL THE TIME HE USES THE LARGE MAGNIFYING GLASS. HE PUTS HIS HAND THROUGH THE CIRCULAR MAGNIFYING GLASS FRAME, REACHES INTO MAN'S INSIDE POCKETS AND TAKES HIS WALLET.

Great Picture Captions of TV History.

3.2.69/C   69/1083
BBC-2 TELEVISION SERVICE
Q.5.

SPIKE MILLIGAN stars in a new seven-week comedy series, Q.5., which starts on BBC-2 on Monday 24th March.

SPIKE MILLIGAN receiving a drenching in a sketch in episode one.

A BBC-tv COLOUR PROGRAMME

BBC COPYRIGHT· PHOTOGRAPH FROM: BBC, BROADCASTING HOUSE, LONDON W.1.

Victim (*as parson*) And it came to pass, that many come unto the house and, lo, the master took them to the mound and laid his tussock on the water.

Sherlock We must hurry, he's getting worse.

Watson (*almost an echo*) Getting worse he says.

CUT TO STILL OF A CHURCH.

Caption A DE-ORDINATION CHAPEL.

VICTIM ON TABLE UNDER A SHEET. THE SURGEON IS NOW GERMAN, WITH A SHORT GERMAN CREW-CUT WIG. HE HAS TWO HORNS GROWING FROM HIS HEAD LIKE A DEVIL. HE WEARS HEAVY PEBBLE-GLASS LENSES. BY HIM STANDS A NURSE. ADJACENT TO THE NURSE IS THE WIFE OF THE VICTIM. MIDDLE-AGED, JEWISH LOOKING. AT THE HEAD OF THE TABLE STANDS DR WATSON. HE HOLDS A SMALL SOFT BLACKJACK, WITH WHICH HE BELTS THE VICTIM WHEN HE'S CONSCIOUS. DR WATSON NOW WEARS A GERMAN HELMET. VICTIM KEEPS SITTING UP CHANTING.

Victim The lesson for this Sunday will be read by . . .

WATSON BELTS HIM ON HEAD

EVERY TIME VICTIM CHANTS AND RAISES HEAD.

Doctor Zis is the worse case of ordination I've seen since Pope Pius did the Cardinal Wolsey job . . . Quick, nurse, more money!

THE NURSE HOLDS UP A LARGE PIGGY BANK. THE WIFE PUTS MONEY IN. THE DOCTOR REMOVES THE VICAR COLLAR AND FRONT FROM VICTIM WITH FORCEPS.

Doctor Quick, nurse, more money!

THE VICTIM SHOWS THAT HE NOW HAS A WHITE COLLAR PAINTED AROUND HIS NECK AND THE BLACK FRONT PAINTED ON HIS CHEST.

Doctor It's too late, it's taken . . .

JEWISH WOMAN COLLAPSES WEEPING ON THE VICTIM.

Woman Abe – Abe!!!

A POLICE WHISTLE IS HEARD. ENTER KNACKER OF THE YARD, WITH A POLICEMAN. THE INSPECTOR GOES STRAIGHT UP TO DOCTOR.

Inspector Sherlock Holmes, I arrest you for impersonating a dismounted German brain surgeon, and wearing the same wig you wore in Beachcomber.

THE NURSE INDICATES THE DOCTOR. THE INSPECTOR

TURNS TO HIM AND SAYS

Doctor I must warn you, Inspector, that anything you say that is funnier than me will be cut out in the edited repeats.

Announcer Here is a newsflash. A man believed to be the Archbishop of Canterbury is holding out in a vicarage in Lewisham. Exactly what he is holding out has not been stated. Police say he is holding an Atheist hostage.

CUT TO OUTSIDE A HOUSE. TWO POLICE CARS ARE PARKED OUTSIDE. POLICEMEN HIDE BEHIND THEM. THERE ARE NOW TWO SHERLOCK HOLMES, BOTH WITH LOUDHAILERS.

Spike (*Holmes* 1) Listen . . . this is Sherlock Homes speaking.

Holmes (*No.* 2) And this is his double.

Holmes 1 Listen, His Double. Will you please keep quiet when I'm acting?

Holmes (*No.* 2) I only spoke because they pay £2.50 more for speaking parts.

Holmes 1 Well, will you stop the parts of you that are speaking. Listen. Archbishop of Canterbury . . . we know you're in there and we know we're out here. Throw out your crozier or we'll send in Roman Catholic policemen.

SHOT OF ARCHBISHOP AT WINDOW. HE IS HOLDING A DUMMY WITH THE HEAD OF MARGARET THATCHER.

Archbishop Listen, copper! I got Margaret Thatcher prisoner . . . one step nearer and she gets ordained.

POLICEMEN RUSH IN FRONT DOOR.

Archbishop You asked for this (*he ordains the dummy*). Listen, blue eyes. Et tuam dedicadum, it servator Christum, Semper fideli, Amen.

SUBSTITUTE REAL LADY FOR DUMMY MARGARET THATCHER.

Thatcher One step nearer and I'll kill myself.

SHE HURLS DUMMY OF HERSELF OUT OF WINDOW. IT FALLS WITH A LONG LOUD SCREAM.

SPIKE RUNS TO BODY OF MRS THATCHER.

Sherlock (*loudhailer*) Mrs Thatcher – are you all right?

Sherlock 2 (*loudhailer*) Mrs Thatcher, I am His Double.

Sherlock (*loudhailer*) Mrs Thatcher, speak to me – She's deaf! (*to camera*) Now you can see what's wrong with the country.

PRICK A BOX

ORGAN: A FEW BUILD-UP CHORDS.

Voiceover   It's something o'clock here in the heart of London's Grotty Wembley studios. Its Prick a Box, and here is your monster of ceremonies, Mogul Thrash, and on the organ, Eric Grinns.

ORGAN. MORE CHORDS, ETC., AS SPIKE ENTERS IN AWFUL SQUARE SUIT, OLD SCHOOL STRIPED TIE, MICHAEL MILES-STYLE HAIR, A BIG NOSE. HOLDS SHEAF OF PAPERS

Spike   Good evening, and welcome to the show. And tonight as you all know is the final of the Drain Brain of Britain.

CUT TO HANDS OF ORGANIST PLAYING CHORDS.

Spike   And one of the finalists is from the Bradford Wives Christmas Pudding Club, and here she is – Mrs Eileen Gibbs.

MORE CHORDS.
ENTER TWIT HOUSEWIFE WHO'S HAD SPECIAL FRIZZ HAIR-DO.

Spike   Hello, and lovely to have you with us. Ha ha ha. (*coy*) Does your mother know you're in wicked London, eh??? Eh?

SOUND: THE SORT OF SOUNDS A CHARABANC OF HOUSEWIVES MAKES WHEN THE DRIVER TELLS THEM A RISQUE JOKE: ALL OHHHHHHS AND GIGGLES.

Spike   Oh, it sounds like you've got some supporters here tonight. Now, ha ha, are you ready to play Prick a Box.

Woman   Yes.

Spike   Yes. Give her a hand.

APPLAUSE. MORE ORGAN CHORDS. CUT TO HANDS.

Spike   Now, here's the first question, and if you answer correctly, ha ha, you'll be on to our three pounds ten treasure trail. Now, are you ready?

Woman   Yais.

ROLL ON TIMPANI, VERY LOW AND OMINOUS, WHEN SPIKE ASKS THE QUESTION. A CLOCK IN THE BACKGROUND STARTS TO TICK.

Spike   Right. What is your name?

Spike   Would you like the question again?

Woman   Yais.

Spike   I'm asking you, Eileen, Eileen, what is your name? Think hard, now, you've only got one hour.

Spike Milligan as the late Michael Miles.

Woman Er . . .

Spike Almost! Eileen, your husband's name is Gibbs, so you must be . . .

Woman (*inspiration*) Married!!

Spike No, listen, your married name, Eileen, is Gibbs. So your name is?

Woman Eileen Gibbs?

Spike Correct.

APPLAUSE, ORGAN CHORDS.

Spike Yes, Eileen Gibbs, and you're half way to the three pounds ten treasure chest. Now, next question. Who is – nervous? – the Queen of England?

Woman Danny la Rue?

Spike No, Eileen, but you're in the right direction. Who is the Queen of England?

Woman Er. I-I don't know.

Spike I don't know is the correct answer!

CHEERS, CLAPPING.

You win a week's free holiday in the lions' cage at Chessington plus . . .

CUT TO CURTAINS DRAWN ACROSS FREE GIFT STAGE. THE CURTAINS PART. THERE IS A GLITTER GOLD-COVERED PLASTIC DUSTBIN.

. . . this glitter gold dustbin, with a week's free rubbish.

ORGAN CHORDS AND CLAPPING.

Spike And now, the finalist in our old twits contest this week is Chelsea pensioner Sgt Squrds. Now, Sgt, how old are you?

Sgt 92.

Spike 92 is the correct answer. So you win the key to Prick a Box (*hands key*). Now for that key I'll offer you ten bob.

Sgt Ten bob? (*Has heart attack and dies.*)

AS HE DIES, MAN SOUNDS GONG. PRETTY DECORATIVE GIRLS LISTEN TO OLD MAN'S HEART.

Girl He's dead.

Spike Hear that folks, he's dead. Give him a big hand.

APPLAUSE, ORGAN CHORDS.

But don't worry. In dying, Sgt Squrd wins this magnificent fibre-glass coffin . . .

SHOWS COFFIN WITH DECORATIVE GIRL.

. . . and a free burial in the sunny South of France, with a woman of his own choosing. Till next week, this is Mogul Thrash saying Goodnight, everybody, goodnight.

CHORDS. AND FADE TO APPLAUSE. OLD MAN GOES TO GET UP. SPIKE PUSHES HIM BACK WITH HIS FOOT.

Home Mortician's Kit

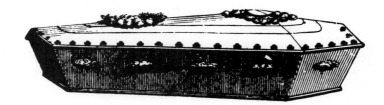

INTERIOR OF GROTTY ROOM. PLASTIC EVERYTHING. AWFUL DECOR. A WOMAN HOUSEWIFE IS HOOVERING.
SPIKE, SECOND SALESMAN (LITTLE CHARLIE) AND THIRD SALESMAN PUSH ON A DOOR ON WHEELS. THEY WEAR DOWDY DOOR-TO-DOOR SALESMEN'S SUITS, TRILBY HATS, SOCKS AND BROWN SHOES. SPIKE HAS FINE PENCIL-LINE MOUSTACHE AND SPECTACLES, WITH HEAVY FRAMES.

Spike   Ah, this must be the place, Tom.

Charlie   It's my turn to knock.

SPIKE LIFTS UP CHARLIE TO KNOCKER: WOMAN ANSWERS DOOR.

Spike   Good morning, madame, I am Mr Herbert Scrackle. Me and my partners want to know if you are prepared for any sudden bereavement.

WOMAN LOOKS.

Spike   Good morning, madame . . .

we want to know if you are prepared for any sudden bereavement.

Woman   Whose?

Spike   A near one, dear one, loved one. Or your husband!

Woman   What's bereavement mean, then?

Spike   Well, kick the bucket. Snuff it.

Woman   A stiff?

Spike   Yes, a stiff. If anyone snuffed it in this house, are you ready?

Woman   What you sellin', shovels?

Spike   No, no. Is your 'usband in?

Woman (*whispers*)   No, no.

Spike   Could I come in and demonstrate?

Woman   Well, if you're quick.

THEY GO THROUGH DOOR, CARRYING THEIR GOODS.

Spike   Now then, supposin' suddenly, tomorrow, in this

delightful settin' one of your loved ones, your 'usband, flakes aht and snuffs it right there on yer carpet. What would you do?

Woman   Go through 'is pockets. . . .

Spike   That's not good enough, madame, think of the neighbours. They wouldn't like to walk in a room and find the wife going fru a dead man's pockets. Oh no. I have here the answer to this delicate problem.

SNAPS FINGERS, AND THIRD SALESMAN STARTS TO UNPACK OR ASSEMBLE THE PORTABLE COLLAPSIBLE LIGHTWEIGHT COFFIN.

It's the GK L098 Home Coffin Kit. It comes in a wide range of colours to match whichever room the stiff is lying in.

Woman   Looks very nice.

Spike   It *is* very nice.

Charlie   Yes. It is very nice.

Woman   Why aren't you at school, son?

Spike   Oh, he's a fully-grown man, but he has the body of a boy of twenty.

WOMAN EXAMINES COFFIN.

Woman   Look, where's he keep it – in the fridge? (*Laughs*, *then serious*) I think this is a bit darft, there's only me 'usband in this house and

he's young and fit, well he was last night.

Spike   Ah, but it's best to be prepared.

Charlie   It's best to be prepared.

THIRD SALESMAN STARTS TO INFLATE A PLASTIC COLLAPSIBLE CORPSE.

Spike   Yes, you can have this coffin on a modest rental until the sad day occurs. And we throw in free this washable polythene inflatable corpse.

Woman   Ohhh, look at him.

Spike   This way you spend many pleasant hours practising how to lay out your loved one when he snuffs it.

THE WOMAN IS HOLDING THE INFLATED CORPSE.

Woman   Ooh, feels nice.

Spike   Yes, filled with hot water it can make a very comfortable bedfellow on a cold night.

Woman   Ooh. I like him.

Spike   The coffin can also be used as a fireside bath. Or in the garden a paddle pool for the kids. Now this is a pound extra.

SPIKE PRODUCES HANDHELD MICROPHONE.

Woman   Wot is it?

Spike   It's a microphone built into the coffin lid, and it plays back on two speakers. So, if your loved one

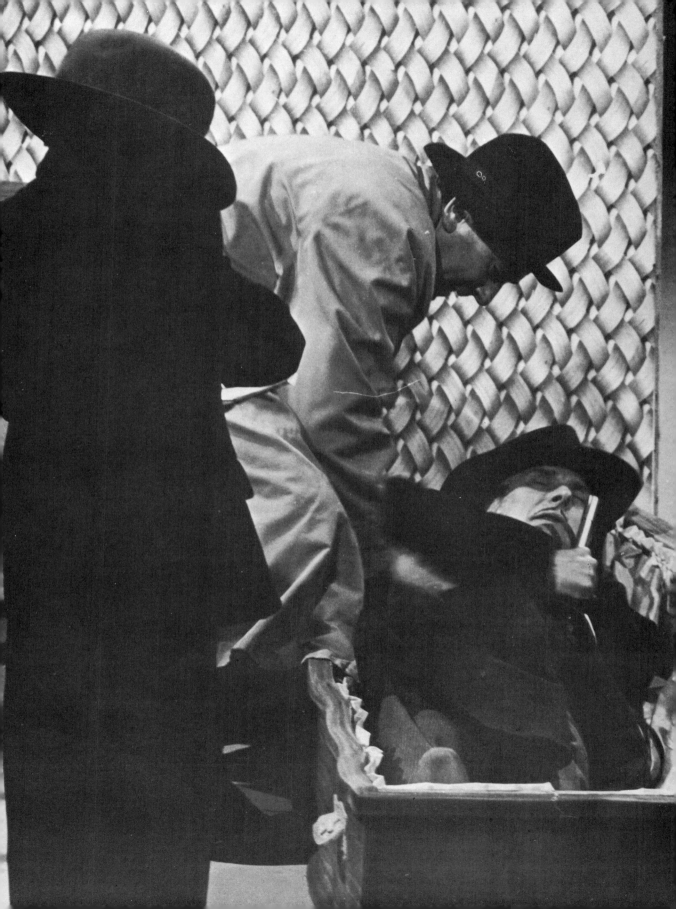

A Fun knee photograph (fun-knee!) (funny!)

is breathin' his larst, you can hear 'im in full stereo all over the 'ouse. Also there's a tape recorder here, so that those that miss the last gasp can hear a repeat the following night.

Woman (*earnest*) I don't want to hear his last gasp all round the house.

Spike Then you . . . AHHHHHH. (*He starts to die.*)

HE HAS A HEART ATTACK AND FALLS NEATLY INTO THE COFFIN AND THE LID FALLS IN PLACE.

Charlie Oh, I fink we've got a sale, Harry.

60

..~:INVENTOR'S CORNER

STUDIO AS FOR A SCIENCE PROGRAMME.

Raymond Baxter Today, electricity has reached out into all our homes. Electricity is now an everyday part of our lives. Here is Mr Furg, the inventor of the electric banana.

Furg This electric banana is long overdue. This banana saves you the problem of having to eat it. In fact, this banana peels and eats itself. So. Also, I have the new electric teeth. This way a man who is tired can sleep and let his teeth do all the eating for him, thus curing night starvation.

Baxter Another brilliant first for England is the invention of the electric leg-crossing machine, invented by Mr Ted Noffs.

Noffs This man is going to have a nap by the fireside. When he is asleep his legs will become uncomfortable, and he would normally have to keep crossing them, not so with the electric leg crosser. Notice every few seconds the electric appliance automatically crosses his legs for him. By fixing the control you can get as many as ten legs crossings in a minute. They can also be straightened out to increase blood circulation.

Baxter Those are just a few inventions that are keeping England ahead of the world. Goodnight.

NEWS DESK

News Reader   And the news. Today the French Ambassador laid a wreath on the Tomb of the Unknown Prime Minister.

This afternoon at Paddington police court, a young lady who gave her name as Miss Whiplash – strict disciplinarian, private massage with correcting fluids – claimed that one of her clients ravished her in lieu of payment.

An American heavily armed bomber on a peaceful mission over Russia accidentally landed on a secret Russian aerodrome, and accidentally took photographs of the installations. The American plane then accidentally took off, whereupon the Russians brutally shot it down. The Americans blame a faulty pilot.

The birth of a child is announced to Lady Rothschild. Mother and child are both doing well, as they hold shares in ICI. The Americans blame a faulty pilot.

Today in the House of Lords, Sir Leslie Grade described Harry Secombe as a nice class of people. Police are taking no action. Secombe blamed a faulty pilot. He also blamed each other.

Two other men are being murdered on suspicion by the police, who are helping them with their burial.

The pound has been devalued for the third time this week. The police suspect a faulty Government.

BBC about to use a laser beam on Milligan in an attempt to bring the series to an end.

HARRY SECOMBE LIQUEFIED

A MAGISTRATES' COURT

Magistrate   Will the prosecution commence?

Spike   Your Worship, it is our intention to prove that negligence by Steam Dick's Turkish Bath and Holding Company Ltd resulted in our client suffering a severe change. It has been said not even his own mother would recognize him.

Mag   Did she ever recognize him?

Spike   No, your Worship – a tree fell on her.

Mag   And how was this change wrought?

Spike   He was reduced from a man of considerable substance to a liquid state.

Mag (*puzzled*)   When you say liquid . . . is he, er, er, dead?

Spike   We don't know, your Worship.

Mag (*agitated*)   What do you mean, you don't know? Either he's dead or he's not dead.

Spike   Begging your Worship's indulgence . . .

Mag   Is he in court?

Spike   Ah . . . in a manner of speaking.

Mag   Then call him.

Clerk   Call Harry Secombe.

Voices   Call 'arry Secombe,

CONSTABLE ENTERS CARRYING A BUCKET.

Mag (*after a pause*)   Are you Harry Secombe?

Constable   No, your Honour, I am Constable Z. Cars, gross take-home pay £18.6.0. with repeats £32.16.4. I just carry the bucket.

Spike   If I could perhaps explain, your Worship. Inside that bucket is the plaintiff Harry Secombe.

Mag   All of him?

Spike   Yes.

Mag   What's he doing?

Spike   Allow me to elucidate . . . On the night of the 1st of April,

64

Peter Jones pondering the effects of Q6 on his married life.

which is by the way of being a Jewish holiday in Morecambe, my client paid a visit to Steam Dick's Turkish Baths. As is usual in such establishments, he was shown a chamber, disrobed, and there left to steam.

Mag   Steam?

Spike   Steam, your Honour. Owing to a faulty valve, the temperature in Mr Secombe's chamber rose to some 800 degrees Fahrenheit, the melting-point of the human body. An attendant rushed in – alas, too late. Mr Secombe now lay in a liquid state on the floor. The attendant, being a sensitive man, mopped him up with a sponge, and wrung him carefully in a bucket – that bucket.

HEAVY OVERACTED MURMURS.

Mag   Silence! I will not tolerate overacting in this court. (Coughs) Can we perhaps see Mr Secombe?

Spike   Constable?

CONSTABLE POURS FROM A BUCKET INTO A TRANSPARENT CONTAINER MARKED WITH LIQUID MEASURE.

Mag   And you are suing for negligence?

Spike   No! We are suing them for short measure. A forensic report states on entering the baths Mr Secombe weighed seventeen stone nine pounds, and gaining all the time. According to this conversion table, Mr Secombe should have been eight and a half imperial pints. I draw the court's attention . . . barely six pints. I need to say no more.

Mag   Very well, say it.

Spike   No more.

Mag   We are saying that Mr Secombe is $2\frac{1}{2}$ pints short!

Spike   Yes . . .

Mag   Can't you top him up with a little tap water?

Couns   No, it's against his religion.

TAKES OFF HIS ROBES, WIG AND FALSE TEETH – HE IS IN PYJAMAS. .

The defence rests!

COUNSEL FALLS FLAT BACK INTO WAITING BED.

DOCTOR'S SURGERY

DOCTOR WITH STETHOSCOPE
AROUND HIS NECK AND HAIRY
MAN ON THE COUCH. DOCTOR
MOVES OVER TO PATIENT WITH
HIS STETHOSCOPE.

Doctor   Yes . . . breathe in . . .
breathe out . . . say Ah . . .

TAKES OFF 'SCOPE AND SHAKES
HIS HEAD.

I'm sorry.

Man   Is it bad, Doctor?

Doctor   Very bad, I'm afraid.

Man   Tell me everything. I'd like to
know the truth.

Doctor   Lady Teazle, your
husband's fears are well founded.
You've suffered a considerable sex
change.

Man   But that's the third time this
week.

DURING THE COURSE OF THIS
DIALOGUE THE PATIENT GETS
DRESSED IN WOMAN'S CLOTHES.
SHE DOESN'T GO BEHIND THE
SCREEN, SHE PUTS THE SCREEN
AROUND HERSELF.

Patient   What causes it?

Doctor   Elephants.

Patient (*horrified*)   I've got
elephants.

Doctor   And worse still, you've got
them low down – where they are
most expensive.

Patient   Are you sure I've got them?

Doctor (*fiddles with microscope*)
Look . . . this is a sample of your
blood.

CUT TO OUT OF FOCUS FILM AS
THROUGH A MICROSCOPE. IT
CLEARS TO REVEAL ELEPHANTS.

Patient   Good heavens!
AT ONE POINT ELEPHANT
LOOKS UP AT CAMERA.

Doctor   Look out! He's seen us.
Run for it.

SOUND OF TWO PAIRS OF BOOTS
RUNNING OUT OF A ROOM AT
GATHERING SPEED.

George V many years before the Q series was made.

CUT TO CHEMIST'S LABORATORY

Chemist   There's no need for anybody to suffer with elephants any more. My company, Eye See Eye to Eye have come up with a brilliant new formula. Here's how to keep your family healthy and elephant-free . . .

CUT TO FILM OF EL ALAMEIN BARRAGE. ROCKET BOMBARDMENT OF IWO JIMA. A NIGHT RAID OF HAMBURG. ATOM BOMB. WHINING SQUADRON. SCREAMING NOISE OF STUKA DIVE-BOMBERS.

And it's only 3s 9d a box.

The Guru

CUT TO STILL OF 'CORONATION STREET' DWELLING AND 'CORONATION STREET' THEME OVER. INTERVIEWER (HUW WHELDON) TALKING OVER.

Huw Don't let this homely facade fool you. Behind this photograph lives the Guru, to give Ned Teeth his full name, who has brought a strange mystic beauty to these otherwise drab surroundings. Her name, the Hon. Lutitia Body, heiress to a car park empire.

INTERIOR OF DRAB AND TASTELESS 1930s HOUSE

Huw Is Ned Teeth your real name, Guru?

Ned No, my real name is Ernesto Shaggnasti Spiroldi Teeth, but I found that a bit of a mouthful – so I shortened it to Ned.

Huw He shortened it to Ned. A name that is redolent of mysticism. Guru Teeth, prior to your finding your higher spiritual manifestation, what were you?

Ned Trainee embalmer at Leith Crematorium. But it's frustrating. There was no outlet for my real talent.

Huw And what is your real talent?

Ned I play 'Abide With Me' on the bones.

Huw And you come from a musical family?

Ned No . . . that's the funny part . . . I don't know where I get it.

Huw So you left the crematorium?

Ned Yes, I like wanted to make the scene, baby.

THE INDIAN MUSIC HAS STOPPED. NED GOES INTO A TRANCE, THEN PICKS UP THE TIN AND PUSHES IT THROUGH THE HOLE IN THE WALL. A COUPLE OF THUMPS ON THE WALL AND THE MUSIC STARTS UP AGAIN.

Huw Guru, for the less knowledgeable, what music is that?

69

Ned That's your mystic Indian raga.

Huw Is it a record?

Ned No, a bunch of wogs in the next room.

Huw You mean coloured colonial gentlemen?

Ned That's right. Real wogs!

Huw How is it that without physical contact you can suggest that you want them to start playing?

Ned Well, you see that 'ole in the wall there. Every half hour I bung a tin of cat-food through. One tin for the ragas and two tins for Sgt. Lonely's Peppered and Curried Hearts.

Huw Later I talked with the Guru's spiritual consort, the Hon. Lutitia Body. How did you contact the Guru?

Lut We met by accident. He ran over me in a dustcart. At the time he was the Assistant Guru to the Hendon Public Cleansing Department.

Huw Was he Jewish?

Lut Yes, he was . . .

Huw And your function now?

Lut I am his handmaiden. I give him my all.

Huw (*turning to camera*) She gives her all. (*Huw turns to Guru.*)

Ned Ours is a relationship, a mutual pattern of giving . . . (*gets chatty*) Sweet girl . . . do you know what she give me the other morning? She trips into me room, gives me a cheque for ten thousand pounds.

Huw And in return?

Ned A receipt.

ENTER MAN IN LONG ROBE BEARING A TRAY WITH FINGER BOWL-TYPE DISHES. THE GURU AND THE GIRL EACH PICK THEM UP WITH BOTH HANDS SCOOPED ROUND THE DISH. GURU AND GIRL CHANT. WE SEE WHELDON GINGERLY LIFT THE CUP TO HIS LIPS AND DRINK.

Huw (*He gives her a receipt*) When in Rome . . .

AND JUST AS HE STARTS TO DRINK, WE SEE THE HORROR IN HIS EYES AS HE REALIZES THAT THE GURU AND THE GIRL ARE WASHING THEIR HANDS IN THEIRS.

Ned 'Ere that's the washing-up water.

Huw That *was* the washing-up water. You see the pitfalls that befall the uninitiated.

Ned Oh . . . Oh . . . that's your kick, is it? Drinking Fairy Liquid . . . freak out, baby . . .

Man in robe Let me explain. The Guru is doing his ritual hand

Spike Milligan measures Napoleon for half a coffin.

washing in anticipation of smoking.

Ned   I'll tell 'im (*he produces a piece of grotty paper and three crumpled cigarettes*). 'Ere, want a trip?

JUST HANDS THEM ROUND. MAN AND GIRL WORSHIP THEM AND HUW WHELDON TAKES ONE.

Huw   What are they?

Ned   Woodbines.

Huw   There we must leave Guru Teeth and his flock. If you have any communications for the Guru.

HE HOLDS UP CARDS READING 'SWAMI NED TEETH, 13A TARIQ ALLEY, JUST OFF THE LETSBE AVENUE, ENGLAND, NW3'.

Announcer   There we leave the Guru, a man of many religious convictions . . . three of which are pending.

71

Beachey Head

A CLIFF EDGE. MAN STANDS POISED ON THE EDGE LOOKING AT ANOTHER MAN IN FULL EVENING DRESS SEATED AT PIANO ON CLIFF EDGE. HE PLAYS INTRO. MAN BENDS HIS KNEES FOR LEAPING, AND SINGS 'AVE MARIA'. HE JUMPS OVER SIDE OF CLIFF, AND WE HEAR THE VOICE FADING, BUT STILL SINGING STRAIGHT. BY THE END OF THIRD BAR WE HEAR CLUMP OF BODY ON ROCKS.

Commentator   This man was Cedric Lunge, who had signed a contract with a recording company to leap off Beachey Head and sing 'Ave Maria' before he hit the rocks below. He was killed outright. This was a flagrant breach of contract. The company sued the family for the remainder of the song.

So the son, Hercules Lunge, took up the challenge to clear his father's name. Let us recap (*puts on cap*). Cedric Lunge, from Point A, managed to sing three bars of 'Ave Maria' before hitting point B. Contractually he was twenty-nine bars short, and dead. It meant that Hercules Lunge's descent would have to be much slower. His uncle, a guards sergeant with only one conviction, came up with a superb idea. A pair of parachute socks. Several tests were made using a weighted body called Hercules Lunge.

All set, then, for the second attempt.

FILM OF MAN GOING OVER THE SIDE EXACTLY AS BEGINNING, EXCEPT MAN WEARS PARACHUTE SOCKS AND STARTS LATER IN. A COUPLE OF BARS, THEN CRUNCH.

Comm   A fresh breach of contract. The record company was losing its patience. The Lunge family was losing people. However, into the breach has stepped Aristotle Lunge, the great great grandson of Cedric, the first of the singing, jumping and dying Lunges.

FULL HOSPITAL BED WITH PATIENT IN TRACTION AND HEAD SHROUDED. ALONGSIDE STANDS A TRAINER FIGURE IN

72

Spike Milligan as Heathcliff breaks the news to Kate Bush that her record is now available in fish and chip shops – the tandem is a ruse.

PLIMSOLLS AND CAP. SON IS SINGING 'AVE MARIA' ALL THE TIME UNTIL QUESTIONED. HE IS CLOBBERED ON EVERY BAR BY THE TRAINER WITH AN IRON ROD.

Comm   And as you can see, he has broken off his training, both his legs and his neck to be with us tonight. With him is his trainer, Tom Danger. In your own words, Aristotle, tell us what you are doing.

Son   I feel I have a destiny to fulfil.

Comm   Could you elaborate on that?

Son   Yes.

Comm   Tell us how many bars remain of the elusive 'Ave Maria'.

Son   Thirteen.

Comm   Isn't that an unlucky number?

SON LOOKS AT TRAINER FOR ADVICE.

Trainer   Naaa . . . naaa . . . luck is luck. For example, my first wife was killed on the thirteenth of July when a tree fell on her. Two years later, thirteenth of July, second wife killed, tree fell on her. Strewth, thirteenth of July again, having married thrice, she gets killed.

Comm   Don't tell me a tree fell on her.

Arthur   Naa . . . Naaa . . . she died in bed.

Comm   What happened?

Trainer   A tree fell on her . . .

Comm   How are you training Mr Lunge?

Trainer   I set 'im off singing 'Ave Maria' at a fair trot. Then we drop rocks on his head fortissimo ma non troppo.

Comm   What effect does this have on him?

Trainer   A lasting one.

Comm   In other words.

Trainer   There aren't any other words.

Comm   Are you Jewish?

Trainer   No, a tree fell on me. What happens is this, see. The night before, he sleeps with his head in a bucket of brine. The next morning a massage with me own Nerks Nut Nourisher . . . Then we drop rocks on his head. Then he has breakfast.

Comm   Do you think this concentrated dropping of rocks on him will do the trick?

Trainer   No.

Comm   Why do it?

Trainer   I don't like 'im. Time for another work out!

TRAINER SMASHES PATIENT WITH HAMMER AS HE SINGS 'AVE MARIA'.

At the Zoo

SCENE AT THE ZOO, WHERE AN OLD KEEPER IS SCRUBBING DOWN THE ELEPHANT. HE IS SINGING A BOWDLERIZED MUSIC HALL SONG. A VERY REFINED VOICE IS HEARD. THE VOICE HAS AN ENCLOSED SOUND AND A SLIGHT ECHO.

Voice Excuse me.

KEEPER REACTS.

Voice (*more urgent*) Excuse me.

KEEPER WALKS ROUND TO FRONT OF ELEPHANT AND LOOKS IT IN THE FACE. CONTINUES TO SING AND SCRUB ELEPHANT.

Voice Is there anybody out there? Hallo.

Keeper Yes. Where are you?

Voice (*cough*) Inside.

Keeper Inside?

Voice Yes.

Keeper Inside what?

Voice The elephant – I'm inside the elephant.

Keeper (*puts ear against side of elephant*) I don't believe you.

Voice You don't have to believe me. All I want you to do is to make a simple phone call.

Keeper 'Ere, you're having me on. You're not in there. Give a bang.

WE HEAR THE SOUND OF FOUR KNOCKS.

Keeper Walk about a bit.

WE HEAR THE SOUND OF FOOTSTEPS.

Keeper Cor, bloody 'ell. Ow did you get inside, then?

Voice I know the right people.

Keeper (*touching hat*) I'm sorry, sir. I don't want to cause trouble . . . but have you paid to come in?

Voice No.

Keeper I'm sorry, sir, I'll have to call a copper.

KEEPER WALKS OUT OF PICTURE.

Voice (*singing*) 'Someday I'll Find You . . .'

Spike Milligan in 'The World About Us is Bloody Awful' – The elephant is a ruse.

KEEPER COMES BACK INTO SHOT, ACCOMPANIED BY COPPER.

Copper Now what's it all about, Alfie?

Keeper There's a bloke 'ere who got in without paying.

Copper Oh? Where is he?

Keeper He's inside the elephant.

Copper Would you like to say that again?

Keeper Yes, there's a bloke what's got in without paying . . .

Copper And where is he?

Keeper He's inside the elephant.

COPPER JUST HANDS KEEPER A BREATHALYSER BAG TO BLOW UP.

Spike sings Irving Berlin's 'In your Easter Bonnet' to an elephant on Christmas Eve.

Keeper   What's this for?

Copper   I have reason to believe that you are drunk in charge of an elephant.

KEEPER BLOWS UP BAG. COPPER TAKES IT AND SPEAKS.

Copper   I must apologize to you. You are not drunk in charge of an hefelant.

Voice (*inside*)   Are you back yet?

Copper   What was that?

Keeper   It's 'im. The bloke inside the elephant.

Voice   I say. Hallo!

POLICEMAN TAKES OUT A BAG AND BLOWS IT UP HIMSELF.

Keeper   Hallo . . . hallo . . . Listen,

you in there, I've got a copper with me . . . so watch it!

Voice   What do you want to go and do that for?

Copper   This is the constable speaking, sir. I've reason to believe that you got in here without paying, sir, and I'll have to take a few particulars.

Voice   Look, all I want is this. Will somebody phone up Fortnum and Masons and tell them to collect my lawn mower as the axle is out of alignment.

Copper   What is your name, sir?

Voice   I'm not going to give it to you.

Keeper   Listen. Don't mess about. You're inside one of our best elephants.

Voice   I can't hear you.

Keeper (*goes to elephant's trunk*)   Is that better.

Voice   You can't do anything to me. In this position I am completely unassailable.

Copper   'E's right, Alf. I'll have to go and get a search warrant.

Spike   You're for it, mate.

Sid Snot – Punk rocker trying to impress the Queen at a Royal Garden Party.

78

DOCTOR'S SURGERY

THERE IS A HUGE CLOCK ON THE WALL WITH A VERY CLEAR SECOND HAND. AS A PATIENT COMES THROUGH THE DOOR, THE DOCTOR SETS THE CLOCK GOING. BUZZER ON DOCTOR'S DESK BUZZES.

Doc   Yes.

Voice   Lady de Vere Rothschild's here.

Doc   Just a minute, send her in . . .

PUNCHES A BUTTON THAT STARTS THE CLOCK GOING.

. . . starting now.

Lady de Vere   Ah, doctor, doctor I haven't slept a wink for weeks . . . the most dreadful pains in my dog's legs . . .

Doc (*writing furiously*)   Yes, yes, yes . . .

THE CLOCK IS CLEARLY MARKED OFF IN GUINEAS NOT MINUTES.

Lady de Vere   And the most terrible thing is that I know . . .

AND HER VOICE BECOMES A BABBLE PUNCTUATED BY THE TICK OF THE CLOCK, AND THEN FINALLY A LOUD BELL RINGS OUT INTERRUPTING HER.

Doc   I'm sorry, Lady de Vere Rothschild, your time is up. That's all we have time for this week, and you owe me fifty guineas. Can you afford to come back again next week.

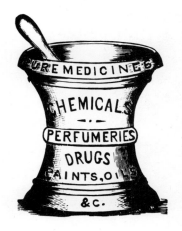

Snobb

Announcer Snobbery . . . the curse of the working class. Or as some would have it, the curse of the working *class*. Is cursing the snobbery of the working class or work the snobbery of the cursing class?

THROWS DOWN A GLASS BALL AND LAUGHS.

Let us describe snobbery. A cut finger . . . bandaged like this . . .

AND WE CUT TO FINGER GROTTILY BANDAGED

Or like this.

AND WE CUT TO FINGER BANDAGED WITH A PRETTY RIBBON

N.B. He didn't get it – neither did she

NAPOLEON
who never even dreamed of the Q series

Now which of these is the snob?
This or this?

AND WE SEE GROTTY FINGER

It is, of course, this.
Why? Because its owner wears a velvet groin appliance for months at a time.

Ann   Another example. Which one of these men is the snob?

TWO MEN IN BATH, ONE AT EACH END, ONE OF THEM WEARS BOWLER.

Man without bowler   I am.

Because I wear a velvet appliance in the baths for months at a time.

Man with bowler   I am not a snob, but I wear a bowler hat in the bath because you never know who might call.

Ann   Well then, what is a snob?

STREET WITH A ROLLS ROYCE CRUISING AND CHAUFFEUR RUNNING ALONGSIDE.

Chauffeur   A snob is a geezer what won't travel in the same jam-jar as his chauffeur.

Lifeguard

FILM OF BLACKPOOL. PROFUSION OF VARIOUS HOLIDAY MAKERS. CANDY FLOSS, ROCK, FUNNY HATS, MUSIC: REGINALD DIXON ON ORGAN PLAYING 'BESIDE THE SEASIDE'.

Voiceover   Tahiti? No, wrong again. It is our own merry Blackpool, a little piece of plaster of Paris in the heart of England.

FILM CONTINUES AND BECOMES RAGING GALES, SMASHING SEAFRONTS. LIFEBOATS LAUNCHING, HELICOPTER RESCUES AT SEA. OIL ON BEACHES.

What is it about this jewelled magnet that draws the Barnsley jet-set back year after year after year. It is the death wish.

CUT TO LIFEGUARD'S HUT

Lifeguard (*inside*)   'oo is it?

Man   There's somebody drowning.

Lifeguard   Ta.

PAUSE

Man   Good morning.

THERE IS A CRY OF 'HELP!'.

Did you hear what I said, I want to report a drowning.

Lifeguard   All right, all right.

COMES TO DOOR. THERE'S A FRESH CRY FOR HELP AS HE OPENS THE DOOR.

Man   You heard that.

Lifeguard (*in pyjamas, picking up milk*)   Yeah . . . you'd better come inside for a minute.

Man   Ins . . . For God's sake, hurry up, man.

Lifeguard (*turning to go in*)   I can't go in there in me 'jamas. They pull you under. Wouldn't look nice on the council plaque. 'Hercules Shand, Lifeguard. Drowned not saving anybody.'

FRESH SCREAM.

Man   Look, never mind about 'jamas. That's my wife drowning.

Lifeguard   Oh.

83

THEY MOVE INTO HUT.

Man Look, I think you're taking a very casual attitude – I mean it's a matter of . . .

DISTANT CRY OF HELP.

Lifeguard Tell her I'm coming.

Man (*turning to window*) He's comi . . . What do you mean you're coming? For heaven's sake . . .

Lifeguard (*now stripping off pyjamas, showing appropriate bathing costume underneath*) Right, where is she?

A HUGE MAP ON THE WALL. IT IS A SEA CHART SHOWING DEPTHS, TIDES, ETC. LIFEGUARD PUTS ON GLASSES.

Lifeguard Now, where is she, which part is she in?

Man (*looks out of window and fixes on chart*) She's about there . . . and she's drifting west.

Lifeguard Right . . . now we're getting somewhere.

LIFEGUARD PUTS FLAG IN TO MARK SPOT, THEN GETS FORM OUT OF DRAWER AND SITS AT DESK. FURTHER SCREAM OF HELP.

Lifeguard What's your wife's name?

Man Squills.

Lifeguard No, maiden name.

Man Do you know . . . good God, this is silly, isn't it? Do you know I can't remember.

DISTANT CRY FOR HELP.

Lifeguard Well, ask her . . . we haven't got time to hang about.

Man Darling . . . what's your full maiden name?

Woman's voice It's Marion Squills. Marion Q. Squills.

Man What's the Q for?

Woman Fish. It's Friday.

MAN RUSHES BACK INTO HUT.

Man Right, come on now, let's go.

Lifeguard Listen, sailor, I know me job. How far do you reckon she's out?

Man Hundred yards.

BEHIND WE HEAR A TERRIBLE AGONIZED SCREAM.

Woman's voice For God's sake, John.

MAN SHUTS THE WINDOW TO CUT OUT SCREAM.

Lifeguard (*starting to measure off lengths of line*) One, two, button me shoe, three, four, marjorie door . . . Wait a minute, where did you say she was?

Man She's there, damn you, there.

Lifeguard (*just drops the rope*) Oh

A normal day in the **Q** series office.

. . . you've come to the wrong bloke, mate.

Man What in God's name do you mean?

CRY OF HELP.

Lifeguard Well, she's drowning between Fred Quimby's groins.

Man Fred Quimby? What are you talking about?

Lifeguard That's where your Mrs is . . . in Fred Quimby's area.

Man But look, you're letting my wife drown.

Lifeguard I'm not letting her drown . . . Fred Quimby's letting her drown. I don't know how he can stand idly by and let a woman drown.

CRY OF HELP.

Man But please, please, can't you save her just this once?

Lifeguard I can't save her. If I did he'd make me throw her back again.

CRY OF HELP, FOLLOWED BY DEEP MALE CRY OF HELP.

Man (*now pleading on knees*) For God's sake . . . I beg you, please . . . just this once . . . my wife . . . she's all I have . . . please save her.

WOMAN DASHES INTO HUT, SHE IS WEARING FULL EVENING DRESS.

Woman Help me, help me, my husband's drowning.

Man Amanda.

WE HEAR THE STRAINS OF 'I'LL SEE YOU AGAIN' CREEPING IN.

Woman Noel.

Lifeguard (*with megaphone*) Mrs Squills, I've got some bad news for you.

Get your margarine on the HP and spread it over two years

CRIMINALS

OUTSIDE A POST OFFICE. WE
SEE MAN COMING OUT OF POST
OFFICE DOOR, DRESSED IN
ORDINARY SUIT, TRILBY AND
RAINCOAT. HE IS APPREHENDED
BY ANOTHER MAN OF A MEANER
JOWL. HE TOO IS DRESSED
NORMALLY. HE HANDS MAN A
CARD.

Voiceover A new type of crime has
come to the West End. The quiet
criminal who operates in a
particularly devilish way.

Criminal Just a minute, sir. I'm a
quiet criminal who operates in a
devilish way. My card.

Man What's this say? 'Louis Tonk,
alias Sir Laurence Olivier, alias
Judi Dench. Professional burglar and
criminal assaults done while you
wait.' I don't understand.

Criminal Look, sir (*opens coat to
show pistol, hatchet, knuckle-
dusters, a club and knives*). This gun
is loaded, sir. And so is the axe. I
have a licence for it. I could rob you
with violence, of course, but I
thought I'd give you a chance.
Cigarette?

Man No, thank you.

Criminal They're yours.

Man I thought I'd given them up.

Criminal I happen to know that
apart from that joke laying an egg,
while you were in the post office you
drew out your child's allowance of
eleven pounds three and a penny.
We'll forget about the odd penny.
Let's get down to business. I could
have stuck you up with this gun,
taken the lot and shot you dead. But
I don't want all that unsavoury
publicity, not with my television
series coming up. And I'm certain
that you don't want any violence on
you, sir.

Man Oh no, certainly not.

Criminal Right, sir, if you'll just
let me have your cheque for five
pounds, you'll be six pounds to the
good.

Man Well, that sounds perfectly
reasonable to me. I get six pounds and
you get five.

MAN TAKES OUT HIS CHEQUE
BOOK.

Florence Nightingale, curing soldiers of the Q series.

To whom shall I make the cheque out?

Criminal   Non-Violent Enterprises Ltd, branches in the Strand.

Man   And could I have a receipt, please, for tax purposes?

Criminal   Oh no . . . that's not all. Our district manager has been casing your joint and he reports a pair of silver candlesticks valued at £80.10.0.

Man   Yes?

Criminal   When would it be convenient for our van to call?

Voiceover   There you see this new insidious brand of criminal at work. Do not give in to this unscrupulous method of robbery. They can be defeated, as in the case of Sir Carrington Briggs who was confronted by these men but sensibly stood his ground. Consequently all his property remains intact. (*Pause*) The funeral takes place tomorrow. It will be televised live from Golders Green Hippodrome.

Courtroom

A COURTROOM. PRISONER IN DOCK. COUNSEL AND JUDGE IN ROBES.

Judge You have been found guilty of first degree murder in the second degree of Thomas Fu, Chinese pianist and Willesden launderette. And to clear up the backlog of unsolved crimes, you have also been found guilty of the brides in the bath murders, the Dorking thigh molester, eighteen phantom chopper attacks and the destruction of London by fire in 1634. What do you have to say?

Prisoner Not guilty.

Judge We know you're not guilty. But there is a productivity drive on, and you are doing your bit to help the country clear up this backlog of court orders. Now what do you say?

Prisoner I didn't do none of it sir.

Judge We'll give you nine prisoners' last breakfast and the top off the milk. Have you any last requests?

Prisoner Yes, sir. 'Just a Song at Twilight'.

Judge Right (*breaks into song*).

THEN ALL THE MEMBERS OF THE COURT JOIN IN. WHEN THE SONG FINISHES THE PRISONER IS IN TEARS.

Prisoner Ta.

Judge Take him down. Next . . .

ANOTHER PRISONER WALKS INTO THE DOCK.

Judge Now, prisoner at the bar, what is your occupation?

Prisoner I'm a recording manager

Judge Oh . . . (*breaks into 'Yesterday'*).

Newsdesk

AT THE NEWS DESK IS SPIKE. BEHIND HIM ON SCREEN IS FILM OF HOUSES OF PARLIAMENT AT NIGHT. STANDING ALONGSIDE ARE FOUR MEN AND ONE WOMAN, ALL DONE UP IN ANCIENT GREEK ANKLE-LENGTH TOGAS. IN ONE HAND THEY CARRY THE GREEK MASK OF TRAGEDY AND IN THE OTHER THEY CARRY THE GREEK MASK OF COMEDY. WITH THE OTHER HAND THEY FEEL THE TOPS OF STOCKINGS.

Spike Good evening. Here is the news with the BBC Greek chorus. There has been a major earthquake in Asia Minor.

CHORUS MOANS, PUTS UP SAD MASK.

In Turkey, a girl of sixteen married a man of ninety-two. The funeral took place at the Mosque of St Omar, Istanbul.

CHORUS STIFLE THEIR LAUGHTER.

A prizewinning golden labrador, Hoxton Beauty, has given birth to sixteen puppies.

WOMAN GOES 'AAHHHHAH'. ALL THE MEN TURN TO LOOK AT HER IN BEWILDERMENT.

Finally, an entrant in the Miss America contest gave a bust measurement of forty-four inches.

GREAT GROANS OF LUST FROM THE MEN.

Spike Milligan conducting the Boston Symphony Orchestra outside a Pizza Bar in Acton.

Constable Mrs Stella Pudding, we have an extradition order for you.

ALL THE COPPERS CARRY THEIR OWN BUCKETS OF NATIONAL SOIL, WHICH THEY STAND IN WHEN THEY SPEAK.

Spike I am not Mrs Stella Pudding. I am Ernest Quaint.

Con We also charge you with impersonating Mrs Stella Pudding.

Spike (*jumping into a bucket*) You cannot arrest me.

Con Why not?

Spike I am standing in a bucket of Nationalist Chinese soil.

Chinaman (*issuing forth suddenly from a door*) We had anticipated your move. I allest you for Blank of Engrand lobbely of one plound.

Spike Too late, Chinky poo fiend, I happen to be now standing on a bucket of Free Congolese soil.

Congolese copper I arrest you for being a white mercenary in the Katanga area.

Spike Foiled. Sam Bokins, (*moves into another bucket*), Israel.

Israeli copper Funny you should say that. I arrest you on three charges. But to you, two.

Spike Ah . . . (*another bucket*) Pakistan.

Pakistani copper I am Saramatool Curry. I arrest you for disturbing the piece of Pakistan.

Spike What peace?

Pakistan That piece you're standing on.

Spike None of you will capture me!

THERE IS A LARGE GLASS TANK FULL OF WATER AND PLASTIC FISHES – SPIKE RUNS UP LADDER, JUMPS IN UP TO HIS NECK.

Spike Safe again! This sea water came from outside the English six-mile limit.

IMMEDIATELY A MAN RUNS UP LADDER BEHIND HIM, HANDS HIM A PORTABLE RADIO WHICH IMMEDIATELY STARTS TO PLAY POP MUSIC.

Man I am the Postmaster General, and I accuse you of being a pirate radio station. What have you to say?

92

 Spike Milligan – ace dog-killer

Snobs

Spike Are we a nation of snobs? To what extremes will we go to be accepted as upper class. Let's try an experiment. Mrs Deborah Fuchs, 23 Grouters Lane, Neasden, is our guinea pig.

SPIKE PUTS ON POSTMAN'S HAT, PICKS UP PARCEL FROM DESK AND WALKS ACROSS TO THE SCENE.

Spike Mrs Fuchs?

Woman Yes.

Spike Parcel. Special delivery.

Woman Ooh . . . I wonder what it is?

Spike It's on the label here, madam . . . it's horse manure.

Woman 'Orse manure . . . I didn't order any 'orse manure. (*Jokily*) You'd better take it back to the horse. There must be some mistake.

Spike There's no mistake about 'orse manure, madam. I knew what it was the moment they put it on the van.

Woman I'm not having it.

Spike It's nothing to do with me. I'm just a postman. I'll be glad to get rid of it, if you must know. We're freezing to death having to drive the van with the window open.

Woman Who's it from?

Spike It's on 'ere, madam. With the compliments of Her Majesty the Queen, Buckingham Palace, London, S . . . W . . . 1.

Woman (*looks and smiles slowly, realizing*) The Queen?

TAKES PARCEL AND LOOKS AT LABEL.

Woman   You're right. Well, beggars can't be choosers.

SHE WALKS BACK INTO HALL.

John, a great honour has been visited upon us.

John   What is it?

Woman   You'll never guess.

SPIKE WALKS TOWARDS CAMERA, TAKES OFF POSTMAN'S HAT.

Spike   The question to ask yourself is this: Would you accept an unsolicited parcel of horse manure from the Queen?

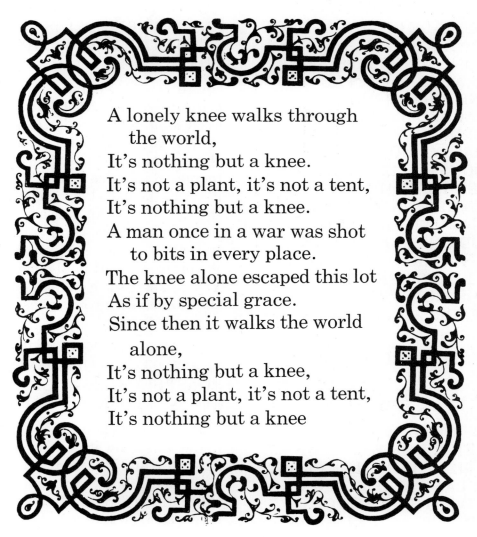

A lonely knee walks through
    the world,
It's nothing but a knee.
It's not a plant, it's not a tent,
It's nothing but a knee.
A man once in a war was shot
    to bits in every place.
The knee alone escaped this lot
As if by special grace.
Since then it walks the world
    alone,
It's nothing but a knee,
It's not a plant, it's not a tent,
It's nothing but a knee

BERMUDA TRIANGLE

SPIKE IS SEATED AT A DESK THAT IS MADE OF LIPTON'S TEA CHESTS. A WHITE RABBIT IS ON TOP MUNCHING GRASS. SPIKE WEARS A SOLAR TOUPEE AROUND HIS FOREHEAD. FROM IT ATTACHED BY STRING ASCENDING SKYWARDS ARE SEVERAL COLOURED BALLOONS FILLED WITH LIGHTER-THAN-AIR GAS. BEHIND HIM, TWO MEN ARE HOLDING OUT A RATHER RAGGED UNION JACK. ONE WEARS A UNICORN'S HEAD AND ONE A LION'S HEAD. THE MOUTHS ARE OPEN SO THAT THE ACTOR'S FACE CAN BE SEEN.

THEY HUM 'LAND OF HOPE AND GLORY' IN THE BACKGROUND, AND MAKE THE FLAG FLUTTER GENTLY AS IN A BREEZE. IN CENTRE OF FLAG IS A CUT-OUT HOLE, THROUGH WHICH WE SEE GIRL WEARING THE CROWN OF ENGLAND AND GRINNING (ONE TOOTH BLACKED OUT). SPIKE WEARS A SHIRT MADE OUT OF NEWSPAPER. A FUNNY CLOCKWORK DOLL IS WALKING ACROSS THE TOP OF THE TEA CHESTS.

Spike   Good evening. (*Holds up grin stick with one tooth missing*) According to the *Radio Times* this show is called Q7. Aren't they clever. This year, the *Guardian* increased its price to 15p. That took it out of the fish shops and on to the smoked salmon counter at Harrods – or as it's now called, Harrabs. Let me read from it. May the ninth. Q6 – oddball comedy show. Yes, folks, it's the oddball comedy show, and you have to guess which one of us has it.

REACHES DOWN AND ON A PLATE BRINGS UP A WHOLE ROAST SUCKLING PIG. SETS IT DOWN BEFORE THE RABBIT.

Come on! Eat yer dinner. Did you know, this show is not seen in Australia and New Zealand? Remember, there's an Immigration Office in the Strand. Here's a very nice letter, I'd like to read it. (*He*

MIDGET. What are you laughing at?
FANNY. Something outside of this photograph.

reads it) Thank you. (*He picks up an orchestral Triangle and reads.*) Made in Bermuda? Ahhh! This is the dreaded Bermuda Triangle, at the touch of it I will disappear. (*Strikes it. He doesn't disappear. So he starts to walk sideways out of shot.*) Look I'm disappearing . . . (*Ad libs – What's gone wrong?*)

MONTAGE OF NEWSPAPER HEADLINES. "BERMUDA TRIANGLE SHOCK HORROR". "DAILY EXPRESS DISAPPEARS WITHOUT TRACE IN BERMUDA TRIANGLE", "PYTHAGORAS HAS THEORY ABOUT BERMUDA TRIANGLE SHOCK HORROR", "WORLD DISAPPEARS IN BERMUDA TRIANGLE", "BERMUDA TRIANGLE DISAPPEARS IN BERMUDA TRIANGLE", "DAVID FROST INTERVIEWS BERMUDA TRIANGLE".

CUT TO A TRAVEL AGENTS IN A STREET. ZOOM IN TO SHOW SIGN "EXCITING BERMUDA TRIANGLE TOURS LTD. DISAPPEAR WITHOUT TRACE FOR FOURTEEN DAYS. REGISTERED OFFICES: STAND 'G', WATFORD FOOTBALL GROUND.

DISSOLVE INTO INTERIOR OF ONE OF THOSE "JUST KEEP GOING" TRAVEL AGENTS. VERY SMALL AND CRAMPED. ON THE COUNTER IS A BELL. ON THE WALL BEHIND ARE SEVERAL GROTTY POSTERS: "MAJORCA – 14 DAYS FOR THREE POUNDS. GIBRALTAR – FREE FOR ONE YEAR. SEE YOUR RECRUITING DEPOT. BRADFORD RIVIERA – TEN SUNLESS DAYS IN THE NORTH: £5. BEHIND THE COUNTER SITS A MAN WHO WEARS WHAT WAS A TRENDY SUIT BUT IS NOW WOEFULLY CRUMPLED AND WORN. HE HAS TWO BITS OF PAPER STUCK TO BLOOD SPOTS WHICH HE CUT WHEN SHAVING. HE SITS FOR A LONG TIME SAYING NOTHING.

CUT TO FULL SCREEN CAPTION.

WE APOLOGISE FOR THIS LOSS OF SOUND. THE ACTOR'S MEMORY WILL BE RESTORED AS SOON AS POSSIBLE.

ENTER SPIKE AND RITA WEBB AS MIDDLE-AGED TOURISTS. SPIKE GOES TO COUNTER, AND RINGS BELL THAT IMMEDIATELY GOES THROUGH THE TOP OF THE COUNTER.

Travel Agent Was that you ringing?

Spike No, it was the bell. We wish to complain about our luxury three pounds for twenty days' holiday in the Bermuda Triangle.

Agent Complain? Why, what went right?

Spike Everything, didn't it, Rita?

Rita My name's Molly.

Spike Of course . . . I was thinkin' of *her*. (*Looks up*)

IMMEDIATELY A PHOTO STILL OF A PAIR OF LARGE WELL-SHAPED BOOBS APPEARS JUST TO THE RIGHT ABOVE HIS HEAD.

Agent (*form filling*) Are you two married?

Spike No, just practising.

Rita Well, he's got a long way to go, then.

Spike Please, Molly. Our sex life should be kept quiet.

Rita Then why don't you oil those squeaking bedsprings, then?

SPIKE PAUSES, LOOKS AT HER.

Spike (*to agent*) We've lost lots of money over this trip.

Stella Tanner as Eva Braun (Mrs. Hitler) – also as Marlene Dietrich,
Artur Rubenstein, and the all-night Laundromat in Acton.

Agent (*with pencil and pad*) Precisely how much?

Spike Precisely, er, oh, lots. Confidentially, I've booked three flights for her over the Bermuda Triangle with the guarantee of her disappearing without trace. And each time she's come back to the washateria – like a homing sock. I want you to honour your guarantee to make her disappear for ever in the Triangle. Then I'll go back to her.

Agent You don't want the Bermuda Triangle. You want the eternal one!

SPIKE BLOWS RASPBERRY

Agent I see. (*confidential*) Look, sir, married women are not allowed to disappear in the Bermuda Triangle unless they are accompanied.

Spike All right then, I'll get Mrs Mills to play for her.

Agent No, it's got to be the husband.

SPIKE LOOKS AT CAMERA. OVERACTING. TAKES KNOTTED HANDKERCHIEF OFF HEAD. WE HEAR DISTANT STRAIN OF WAGNER'S 'TANNHAUSER'.

Spike I've got to get rid of 'er. I've had ten years of hell with her, followed by thirty years of marriage.

I tell you, there's nothing left of me below the waist. All right then – oogghhhhh. I will go with her.

Spike (*feeling for money*) First I will sing a farewell to my love. (*sings*) The hills are alive with the sound of music (*exits*).

CUT TO TUBE TRAIN. INSPECTOR ENTERS, DRESSED AS LONG JOHN SILVER WITH A STUFFED PARROT ON HIS SHOULDER. HE WEARS, A LONDON TRANSPORT INSPECTOR'S HAT WITH SKULL AND CROSSBONES ON THE FRONT. HE CARRIES A CRUTCH AND BENDS ONE LEG, AS THOUGH IT WERE MISSING.

Inspector Ahoy, me hearties, tickets please. Disaster tickets, please.

Spike Look, it's Long John Saliva, the spitting image of his dad. (*Moves to inspector confidentially*) Inspector, I want to get off.

Inspector Avast, ye lubber (*punches parrot*). No one gets off the Bermuda Triangle disappearance special until book sales have reached five million and (*looks towards camera as though looking out of train window*) we've only just passed the two million junction.

£ £ £ £ £ £ £ THE BANK MANAGER £

A HIGHLY POLISHED BRASS PLATE ON A DESK. IT READS 'M.J. SHYLOCK, MANAGER NAT-WEST BANK' PULL BACK TO REVEAL SUMPTUOUS OFFICE. THE MANAGER WEARS A BLACK JACKET, STRIPED TROUSERS AND PLIMSOLLS. HE WEARS HIMMLER-TYPE GLASSES AND HAS HEAVILY POMADED HAIR. HE WEARS A SILVER-COLOURED CRAVAT WITH A GOLD STICK PIN WITH A SWASTIKA ON THE HEAD OF IT. THE ASSISTANT BANK MANAGER COMES IN. HE WEARS A PERFECTLY NORMAL BLACK JACKET AND STRIPED TROUSERS, BUT IS MADE UP TO LOOK EXACTLY LIKE HITLER.

Assistant Bank Manager   Excuse me, my lord. A Mr and Mrs Dire Poverty to see you.

Manager (*very Noel Coward*)   Well, what do they want?

Asst   A bank loan.

MANAGER LAUGHS HYSTERICALLY AND ASSISTANT JOINS IN.

Manager   Look, it's the Queen's Jubilee Year, send them to Buckingham Palace.

Asst   They've been there. She's sent them here.

Manager   She's getting cleverer every day. They want to borrow money, you say?

Asst   Yes, I've already said it.

MANAGER GETS UP, GOES TO COATRACK, PUTS ON ABOMINABLY RAGGED OVERCOAT AND CAP WITH PEAK HANGING DOWN ONE SIDE.

Manager   Right, send in the clowns.

ENTER SPIKE, DRESSED EXACTLY THE SAME AS MANAGER, AND HIS SHABBY WIFE.

Manager   I'm sorry to have kept you waiting.

Spike   That's all right, Your Majesty, it's only been three years.

Manager   Three? With interest, that'll be four.

WHILST SPEAKING, HE CALCULATES ON A SMALL HANDHELD CALCULATOR.

Manager   Now, do you smoke?

Spike   Yes.

Manager   I'll make a note of that (*writes in notebook*). He smokes. Now, any other extravagances?

Spike   Extravagances? (*laughs*)

Manager   God, I admire people who can laugh in the face of poverty. And you have a face of poverty. Now I must tell you, the banks have had a bad year. Our gold holdings are down to a mere one hundred and fifty-eight million pounds.

Spike   Oh dear, I am sorry to hear that.

Wife   Look, we need money.

Manager   Money! (*Holds chest as though stricken with a heart attack*).

Spike   It's not much. You see, tomorrow is her fiftieth birthday. Can't you help?

Manager   Of course (*he opens what looks like a large cheque book and sings from it*). Happy birthday to you, Happy birthday to you, Happy birthday dear Ada Terrible, Happy birthday to you.

Spike   But what I need is enough to buy her a celebration din-din.

Manager   Din-din? Your current account is overdrawn by 18p and you only have 34p in your deposit account.

Spike   Well what do you advise, Your Majesty?

Manager   Save! Now, how much do you want to deposit?

Spike   Oh, we can't afford to put anything in.

Manager   And I'll tell you something else: you can't afford to take anything out (*pause*). Worse, you can't afford to take *her* out.

Wife   Well, what about this celebration dinner?

Manager   I'm sorry, I won't be able to make it.

Spike   We don't want you to make it. Wogs will do the cooking.

Manager   Look! Remember you're English, you can't afford to eat. Help your country, give it up, and die as soon as possible.

SPIKE MOANS.

Spike   But it says here in 'The Sun' (*he holds up a newspaper which is wrapped round a cabbage, starts to revolve it and reads*): Bank rate down to nine per cent. Good news for small borrowers.

Manager   But you're not small borrowers, you're nearly five foot ten.

Spike   We only want to borrow enough to go to the place. (*Rips off

Spike Milligan's dressing room.

piece of paper from the cabbage and hands it across to manager.)

Manager   What's this? A night of Oriental bliss at the Acton Currydrome – complete one-course dinner: five pounds – food extra (*slams fist on table*). Are you mad?

Spike   Look, supposing we cut out the rice. We could come out under four knicker.

Wife   Yes, that's how he got out of the army.

Manager   Look, in the state you're in you can't even afford knickers. These are hard times.

Spike   You think we don't know? She's been boiling the dinner plates to make soup.

Manager   I'm sorry. The answer is no.

Spike Milligan changing from Batman to Quasimodo via the Lone Ranger on a 137 bus to Uxbridge.

WIFE BURSTS INTO TEARS AND SOBS. SPIKE STANDS UP AND OPENS COAT TO REVEAL MEDALS. HE WEARS TWENTY VCs IN THREE ROWS.

Spike   Do you know what I got those for?

Manager   I'd say about ten bob the lot.

WE HEAR THE DISTANT SOUND OF BUGLE PLAYING 'THE LAST POST'.

Spike   Mons, The Somme, Ypres, Ovaltinie.

MANAGER CHANGES.

Manager   You didn't tell me you were an Ovaltinie (*turns back lapel of coat to reveal an Ovaltinie badge*). Squing squong, squaggle squaggle squoo.

Spike (*sings*)   Yim bom yim bom yim bom bala boo.

Together   We are the Ovaltinies, Little girls and boys.

Manager   Of *course* we can help with this banquet. (*Gets stern again*) But you must keep the cost below *four* pounds.

Spike (*whispering to wife*)   There goes the mango chutney, darlin'.

SPIKE AND WIFE EXIT.

Manager   Another happy ending, thanks to the big four. See your friendly Bank Manager today. With us you go straight from Bankers Card to –

THERE IS A SOUND OF POLICE CAR APPROACHING.
SPIKE DIVES UNDER THE DESK.

Spike   Some fools say that "Do it yourself" doesn't work. Right, the room's all sparkling and fresh for any visitors now.

HE IS SQUIRTING FRESH AIR AEROSOL CAN INTO ROOM. PAUSES, LOOKS AT WIFE. GOES BEHIND HER AND GIVES HER A GOOD SQUIRT. READS THE SIGN ON THE AEROSOL.

Spike   Ain't that lovely? Rose of England Fresh Air made in Korea. Ah well, I might as well give a touch of the mystic east to myself. *Squirts aerosol down trousers.* I see 'Crossroads' will be on soon. Get ready to switch it off. (*Starts to sing*) 'Sally, Sally' etc. What do you think of that, Doris?

Stella   Of what?

Spike   That tune. (*Sings 'Sally' again.*)

Stella   That's forty years old.

Spike   Don't worry, I'm going to update it.

Stella   How?

Spike   I'm going to call it 'Don't Cry For Me, Argentina'. (*Sings*) 'Sally, Sally, don't cry for me Argentina', see.

Stella (*aside*)   I'll be glad when World War Three comes and he's off again. With a bit of luck, I'll get the widow's pension this time.

GIRL COMES OUT OF THE BEDROOM DOOR, TARTING HER NAILS UP. SHE WALKS ACROSS THE ROOM FROM THAT DOOR TO THE STREET WINDOW. SHE IS SINGING 'ALL THINGS BRIGHT AND BEAUTIFUL' TO HERSELF.

Spike (*watches her*)   'Ere, who's that?

Stella   Oo? It's our daughter.

Spike   Oh *blast*! Just my luck.

Julia   'Ere, Dad, there's an Arab chief pulling up outside.

Spike   Oh, what's he pulling up.

Julia   He's in a white Rolls Royce.

Spike   'Ere, I was at Alamein. I

Spike Milligan – early army days, being forcibly downgraded in the B 4 downgrading chamber.

know all about wogs, I've seen what they can do to the side of a road. Nivea, if you want to save your skin, cover up your revealing parts – and with you that's most of it.

SPIKE RUSHES TO THE WINDOW AND PUTS TELESCOPE TO HIS EYE.

WE SEE A WHITE ROLLS PARKED BY THE PAVEMENT OUTSIDE GROTTY TERRACED HOUSE. TWO ARABS IN FULL TRADITIONAL COSTUME ISSUE FORTH. THEY GO TO THE BOOT.

CUT TO NEW ANGLE WHICH SHOWS A POLICEMAN (SPIKE) STANDING BY THE ROLLS. THE ARABS TAKE THE DUSTBINS AND EMPTY THE RUBBISH ALL AROUND THE POLICEMAN.

Spike Just a minute now, sir. You have just broken the environmental rules of Great Britain – a very serious crime.

ARAB POINTS TO A CD PLATE ON THE DUSTBIN AND THE DUSTBIN LID.

Arab Diplomatic immunity.

Spike I'm afraid that won't save you, sir.

ARAB PUTS A STACK OF FIVERS INTO SPIKE'S HAND.

Spike Now, that'll save you, sir. I'll just go and find some English people to blame.

THE ARAB PRINCE HAS GOT OUT OF THE CAR IN THE MEANTIME. HE GOES UP TO SPIKE, MUTTERS SOMETHING IN COD ARABIC AND BLOWS ENORMOUS RASPBERRY IN SPIKE'S FACE.

Spike That'll be perfectly all right, sir.

UPSTAIRS ROOM – SPIKE STILL AT WINDOW.

Spike Good heavens, those Arabs have dumped all their crap on the pavement. The dirty devils. That's our place for dumping the crap. 'Ere, they're coming up the stairs. It must be the ad – I'd better make myself presentable. The question is – how?

ARAB PRINCE RUSHES IN, FOLLOWED BY HIS TWO ARAB HEAVIES WITH MACHINE GUNS. HE POINTS TO THE DOOR AND HURLS OUT A STREAM OF ARABIC, ENDING WITH THE WORD 'QUICKLY'. THE ARABS FIRE A BURST INTO THE LOCK. THE DOOR FALLS INWARDS RIGHT OVER SPIKE, WHOSE HEAD GOES THROUGH THE CENTRE PANEL – THE REST OF THE DOOR FALLS TO THE GROUND.

Spike Come in, gentlemen. Welcome to Lewisham.

Arab Prince You're welcome to it

too. I am Sheik Machmoud Ishfahan Kalil Gibran Addullah the Seventh. (*He makes prolific Islamic gestures – touching forehead, lips, heart – of greeting.*)

Spike   I'm Dick! (*Crosses himself*)

Sheik   Infidel! (*He spits*)

Stella   'Ere, that lino was new only last year.

Sheik   Diplomatic immunity.

Stella   No it's not, that's gob.

Sheik   Now, white scum, are you the infidel that is advertising building land and ladies' black underwear in the Mecca Daily Express.

Spike   Oh yes. Let me show you around the estate.

SPIKE TURNS HIS BACK TO CAMERA, REVEALING SHATTERED BACK VIEW.

Sheik   And they say they don't need help.

SPIKE TAKES THEM TO THE WINDOW AND POINTS AT THE WINDOW-BOX.
THERE ARE A FEW BITS OF DEAD GRASS, A FEW DOG-ENDS AND A VERY BADLY ERODED PLASTIC YELLOW CROCUS.
THERE IS A PAUSE AS THE ARAB PONDERS WHAT IT ALL MEANS.

Sheik   What is it?

Spike   We keep telling you, it's gob.

Spike Milligan in an arrangement by Richard Rodney Bennett – seats in all parts – even during the performance.

Shiek   No. (*Points to window-box*)

Spike   This is the prime inner London building land.

Sheik   Building land?

Sheik   The exalted one says is this all there is?

SPIKE TURNS TO STELLA.

Spike   Tell him there's some more in a bucket in the karzi.

Wife (*To Sheik*)   Ich haben ein nudder in das kellar.

Sheik (*to Spike*)   What does she say?

Spike   She says *will* you *stop* gobbing on the carpet.

THE SHEIK IS NOW LEANING OUT OVER THE WINDOW BOX.

Sheik   It's very small for building land.

Spike   Small? Until recently, that supported a herd of reindeer.

Sheik   What happened to them?

Spike   They fell off.

SLIGHT PAUSE. HE LOOKS OUT OF THE WINDOW.

Stella   The land's also got fishing rights.

Sheik   Fishing? Where is the river?

Spike   I've got some of it here.

SPIKE TAKES AN ORDINARY WATER JUG AND POURS IT INTO A GLASS AND HANDS IT TO THE ARAB.

You'll get the rest, of course, after your initial down payment.

Sheik   Where's the fish?

Spike   In the fridge. We didn't want it to go off before you came.

Stella   That's the famous river Ouse.

Spike   Yes, that is the one that runs into the River Ahs, hence the famous English saying the oohs and ahs (*laughs*). (*To camera*) They don't understand our subtle sense of humour.

AT THAT STAGE THE GIRL COMES BACK INTO THE ROOM. SHE SITS IN A CHAIR DOING HER NAILS. IMMEDIATELY THE THREE ARABS GO INTO A SEXUAL TRAUMA OF GROANING AND CLENCHING AND UNCLENCHING THEIR FISTS.

Sheik   How much is she?

Spike   She's nine stone eight pounds and you can see where most of that is.

Sheik   I'll buy her. (*He rushes across screaming 'Aua Akbar' and goes into a tremendous embrace on floor.*)

Stella   John, I think our Niveas's schooldays are over.

Spike   Look, I'd better stop him or he'll get a lump in his groin. Stop that, sheik.

Stella I'll get a bucket of water.

Spike Stop this, or I shall call the vice-squad.

Sheik No good. (*He opens his robe and shows a* CD *plate where his sporran would be.*)

SHEIK IMMEDIATELY TAKES GIRL THROUGH DOOR TO BEDROOM.

HALF AN HOUR LATER. SPIKE AND STELLA ARE NOW IN THEIR PYJAMAS, SITTING OUTSIDE THE BEDROOM DOOR ON KITCHEN CHAIRS. WE HEAR THE SOUND OF GIGGLING, AND MANIACAL MALE LAUGHTER AND THE TWANGING AND SNAPPING OF BEDSPRINGS. TWO ARABS STANDING AT BEDROOM DOOR WITH GUNS.

SPIKE IS PLAYING A FOUR-STRINGED BANJO, TUNED AS A UKELELE. HE SINGS 'DONT CRY FOR ME, ARGENTINA'.

Stella Don't play that so loud.

Spike Well, I don't want the neighbours to hear what's going on in there.

Stella Well, I do. It's a change to hear our bed squeaking again.

SPIKE LOOKS DESPAIRINGLY AT CAMERA.

COLOSSAL NOISE COMING FROM THE BEDROOM OF RUNNING FOOTSTEPS. A GIRL IS BEING CHASED BY A MAN IN HOBNAILED BOOTS. MALE MANIACAL LAUGHTER, SCREAMS OF FEMALE. SMASHING OF FURNITURE AND BREAKING GLASS. LOUD EXPLOSION FROM INSIDE ROOM.

DOOR OPENS. OUT STEPS A MIDGET SHEIK.

Spike 'Ere, 'e's overdone it.

The Irish Atom Bomb

DERELICT RAILWAY STATION. THERE IS A LONE IRISH LABOURER WAITING. HE CARRIES PICK-AXE AND ROLLED NEWSPAPER.

Caption HE MUST HAVE MISSED DE LAST TRAIN.

Station Master Well, if he didn't he certainly has now.

Labourer Please speak slower, I'm Irish.

Station Master What are you waiting for?

Labourer I'm waiting for you to speak slower.

Station Master Never mind dem slick English jokes, what train are you waiting for?

Labourer De next one.

Station Master Then you've missed it, it's just gone. And dis is not a railway station, dis is an atom bomb station.

Labourer Den I'll wait for de next atom bomb.

LABOURER AND STATION MASTER ARE ON PLATFORM. THE LABOURER EXPLODES IN A COLOSSAL CLOUD OF SMOKE.

Station Master Oh, he's dead on time.

A HORSE-DRAWN WAGGON PULLS UP OUTSIDE STATION. INSCRIBED ON THE SIDE IS THE WORD 'POLISE'.

Caption THE IRISH ATOMICK COMMISSION ARRIVE.

AN IRISHMAN IN ANIMAL SKINS AND SAXON LEG BINDINGS AND POLICEMAN'S HELMET CARRIES HUGE CLUB. HE DESCENDS FROM DRIVING SEAT.

Caption ATOMICK SECURITY GUARD.

WE SEE BACK OF POLICE WAGGON. THERE IS A THREE PIECE BAND – BAGPIPES, DUSTBIN LID AND HANDHELD HARP – IN MID-SHIN KILTS, HUGE GLENGARRIES, VESTS, BRACES AND PLIMSOLLS.

SPIKE. This show is in colour – why are we in black and white?
DRESSER. It's for the poor people sir.

Caption   MASSED BAND OF IRISH ARMY.

SECURITY GUARD WALKS IN, CLIMBS INTO BACK OF CART AND THROWS OUT RAGGED MALE DUMMY, WHICH GOES OUT OF SHOT. SECURITY GUARD APPEARS AT DOOR WAVING FIST.

Guard   Don't let me catch you drinkin' de heavy water again, Einstein.

DUMMY IS NOW REPLACED BY SPIKE. HE WEARS CRUMPLED BLUE SERGE SUIT, WHITE SHORTS AND TIE. HE IS ON THE GROUND. HE SITS UP AND SPEAKS.

Spike   Einstein? My name's O'Reilly.

SECURITY GUARD WALKS INTO SHOT AND HITS SPIKE OVER THE HEAD WITH THE CLUB.

Caption   PROFESSOR O'REILLY IS GIVEN SECURITY CLEARANCE.

CLOSE-UP OF WOODEN SIGN. IT READS: 'IRISH ATOMICK LABORATORY'. IT HAS BEEN SPELLED 'LAVATORY'.
PULL BACK TO SHOW A CRUMMY GARDENING SHED. THERE IS AN EXPLOSION INSIDE. WINDOWS AND DOORS BLOWN OUT. THICK SMOKE EMERGES. FROM IT, TWO CHARRED, BLACKENED IRISHMEN STUMBLE. THEY SHAKE HANDS.

First Irishman   One more explosion like dat, and we'll be dere.

Second Irishman   One more like dat and we'll all bloody well be dere.

First Irishman   Come on, give us a lift to de testing ground.

SECOND IRISHMAN HAS MOTOR CYCLE GOGGLES AROUND HIS NECK. HE PULLS THEM OVER HIS EYES. SPIKE CLIMBS ON HIS BACK. THEY RUN OUT OF SHOT. EXTERIOR OF GROTTY PUB.

Caption   SECRET IRISH ATOM TESTING RANGE, KILBURN.

ANOTHER SHOT OF PUB. THIS TIME FROM A WIDER ANGLE. THERE ARE SEVERAL DRUNKS SPRAWLED AROUND THE PAVEMENT.

Caption   SECURITY GUARDS MAINTAIN 24-HOUR VIGIL.

A HORSE-DRAWN DUNGCART. LARGE PILE OF DUNG IN STREET. THIS IS BEING ADDED TO BY IRISH NAVVY IN CART.

Caption   THE IRISH NUCLEAR PILE.

TWO IRISH LABOURERS STANDING BY DUNG. THEY ARE HOLDING THEIR NOSES.

Caption   THE REACTORS.

CUT TO PICTURE OF PORCELAIN PO ON A TABLE.

Caption   IRISH HEAVYWATER PLANT.

CUT TO GROTTY MONGREL DOG ON PIECE OF TERRIBLE STRING WITH A LIPTON'S TEA CHEST AS A KENNEL. DOG IS BARKING FURIOUSLY.

Caption   HEAD OF IRISH SECURITY SERVICE.

EXTERIOR OF PUB FROM NEW ANGLE.
THE TWO IRISHMEN ARRIVE PIGGY BACK. THEY APPROACH A DONKEY TETHERED OUTSIDE THE PUB. ONE SPEAKS TO DONKEY.

Caption   PARDON ME, MICK, IS DIS WHERE DE ATOM BOMB IS GOING OFF?

First Irishman   We must be getting nearer.

INTERIOR OF PUB.
ALL IRISH EXTRAS. ALL IDENTICAL. FLOOR LITTERED WITH DRUNKS. THE TWO IRISHMEN GO TO THE BARMAN, WHOSE NOSE REACHES JUST ABOVE THE BAR.

First Irishman   Which bar are dey explodin' de atom bomb in?

Barman   In de garden, because it's not rainin'.

CLOSE-UP ON ILL-WRITTEN SIGN: 'KEEP OUT – VIOLENT EXPLOSIONS IN PROGRESS.'

PULL BACK TO SEE DOOR OF KARZI IN GARDEN. STANDING BY IT IS AN IRISHMAN IN BLUE SERGE SUIT, WEARING A WIMPEY HARD HAT. HE IS FANNING THE KARZI WITH A FAN. THE TWO IRISHMEN ENTER, AND ALL THREE CONVERSE TOGETHER. MAN OPENS KARZI DOOR. WE SEE ROUND BLACK BOMB WITH FUSE AND SHAMROCK STENCILLED ON SIDE.

First Irishman   Why is you explodin' it in there?

Man   We don't want the neighbours to know when it goes off.

MAN LIGHTS THE FUSE WITH A BOX OF MATCHES.
THEY ALL PUT THEIR FINGERS IN THEIR EARS AND RUN OUT. CLOSE-UP ON A PAIR OF EYES LOOKING THROUGH A SLIT.

Caption   THREE IRISH OBSERVERS.

PICTURE AS BEFORE.
CLOSE-UP ON EYES LOOKING THROUGH SLIT. PULL BACK TO SHOW IT'S A LARGE LETTER-BOX.

Caption   ATOM-PROOF OBSERVATION SHELTER.

Caption   THE COUNTDOWN STARTS.

PICTURE AS BEFORE OF LETTER-BOX. IN THE TOP RIGHT-HAND CORNER THE WORD

JANUARY APPEARS, FOLLOWED
BY FEBRUARY, MARCH, APRIL,
MAY (THEY APPEAR ONE AT A
TIME LIKE THE ATOMIC CLOCK
COUNTDOWN).

CUT TO KARZI:

ENTER A DRUNKEN IRISH
SINGER WEARING GROTTY
EVENING DRESS AND HOLDING
A SONG-SHEET.

Caption JOSEF LOCKE
ENTERTAINS THE IRISH
ATOMIC SCIENTISTS.

HE TAKES COAT OFF AS HE

GOES TOWARDS KARZI. GOES
INSIDE AND SHUTS DOOR.
COLOSSAL EXPLOSION. SMOKE
STARTS TO DISAPPEAR. SINGER
IS IN RAGS ON THE KARZI. HE IS
STILL SINGING WITH THE
SONGSHEET ON FIRE. IN RUSH
THE TWO IRISHMEN WHO PUSH
SINGER OFF THE SEAT AND
LOOK WHERE THE BOMB
WOULD HAVE BEEN.

First Irishman It's exploded, Mick.
Now we'll never know how it works.

Singer Dat's de first time de act's
gone like a bomb.

CLEOPATRA

TWO EGYPTOLOGISTS. THEY
WEAR KHAKI SHORTS, SHIRTS
AND TOPIS.

BACKGROUND MUSIC IS
MYSTERIOUS, TENSION-
BUILDING MUSIC. THEY ARE
IN A TOMB, EGYPTIAN
HIEROGLYPHICS ON THE WALL.
THERE IS A SARCOPHAGUS.
VERY DUSTY TOP. SPIKE IS
READING THE HIEROGLYPHIC

ON THE TOP WITH A TORCH.

First Egyptologist It's her.
Cleopatra.

Second Egyptologist (*Spike*)
Lifts up lid of coffin, looks in, slams
lid down.

Spike We're too late. She's dead.

Voiceover Yes, it's the Jubilee
Q7 Show. Prosecutable under the
Trades Description Act.

PULL BACK TO SEE THAT THE SCREEN IS ONE OF FOUR TV SCREENS IN A CONTROL PANEL OF A SPACECRAFT. IT IS SURROUNDED BY DIALS AND FLASHING LIGHTS. BEHIND IT IS A WINDSCREEN THROUGH WHICH WE SEE WHERE THE SPACECRAFT IS TRAVELLING. IN THIS CASE, CATFORD HIGH STREET.

JULIA BRECK AND SHEILA STEAFEL ARE SEATED AT THE CONTROLS. BOTH ARE IN SKIN-TIGHT GLITTER TIGHTS, EXOTIC MARTIAN FACIAL MAKE-UP WITH WIGS TO MATCH.

THE MEN ARE SPIKE (AS CAPTAIN DIAMOND) JOHN BLUTHAL IS DOCTOR SCHMOCK. THEY ARE BOTH WEARING STAR TREK COSTUMES – WITH 'GPO' STENCILLED ON THE FRONT AND BACK. JOHN HAS A HUGE PAIR OF OVERLARGE DOCTOR SPOCK EARS.

Spike It's amazing what American Space technology is turning out today. They turned *her* out – they must have been blind.

SPIKE IS MADE UP TO LOOK LIKE GROUCHO MARX. HE ALSO HAS A HUGE OVERSIZE STOMACH.

Spike Everything under control, Skyella?

Sheila Yes, everything's under control and the kettle's on, Captain Diamond.

Spike (*to camera*) Diamond? Will she never say 'die'? What is our position?

Sheila We're just good friends.

SPIKE WALKS OVER TO JULIA. SHE IS HOLDING ONE OF THOSE CHILDREN'S STEERING WHEELS, USUALLY STUCK ON TO DASHBOARD OF A CAR. SHE IS MAKING CHILDLIKE MOTOR CAR NOISES AND GOING 'BEEP BEEP'.

JULIA RETURNS TO HER MOTOR CAR IMPERSONATION.

Spike We start taking off in a minute.

Julia Ooooh, I'll start first.

STARTS STRIPPING BUSINESS AND IS STOPPED BY THE ENTRY OF DOCTOR SCHMOCK. JULIA HAS CONTINUED MAKING MOTOR-CAR NOISES

Spike Shut up! (*pause*) Darling.

FLOOR MANAGER COMES INTO SHOT. HE CARRIES A FOOT LONG BY EIGHT INCHES WIDE ENVELOPE. SPIKE SNATCHES THE SEALED ORDERS.

Spike Now, I'll open the sealed orders. (*He struggles to open it and finds it impossible.*) Wait, I've just remembered what's inside. It says (*makes small hole in top of envelope and looks in*) you are a GPO Television Detector van. You have been disguised as a rocket to avoid detection. Your mission – search out illegal TV viewers. This message will self-destruct.

ON ONE OF THE TV SCREENS APPEARS TOM JACKSON, HEAD OF THE POSTAL WORKERS' UNION.

Jackson Hello, Finchley Post Office calling.

Spike Yes, Finchley PO, what is it?

Jackson What is your exact position?

Spike I'm standing up and the rest are sitting down – we're not sure about her.

Jackson We're ready for your orders.

Spike Right. One prune yoghourt, and a small brown loaf.

Bluthal (*looking at another screen*) Captain – there's a family here watching without a licence.

Spike Well, that's better than watching 'Coronation Street'.

THE PICTURE WE NOW SEE ON THE TELEVISION SCREEN IS A GROTTY WORKING-CLASS LIVING-ROOM. THERE IS A GROTTY OLD TV SET WITH THE MAGNIFIER IN FRONT OF IT. THE HUSBAND WEARS BLUE SERGE TROUSERS, BRACES AND PYJAMA TOP. HE HAS ON CARPET SLIPPERS. HE HOLDS A CLIPBOARD WITH HIS WORDS ON. THE WIFE IS STELLA TANNER. SHE WEARS A FLORAL APRON. IN FACT SHE'S DRESSED LIKE VIOLET CARSON IN 'CORONATION STREET'. SHE COMES INTO THE ROOM CARRYING A WHITE DOG-FOOD BOWL. BY NOW WE HAVE MIXED FROM TV SCREEN IN ROCKET INTO THE ACTUAL ROOM.

Wife What are you laughing at?

Husband The epilogue.

Princess Anne riding at Badminton and not watching the Q series.

SHE PUTS THE DOG'S BOWL AT HIS FEET. LOOKS AT HIM.

Wife   Aren't you going to eat it?

Husband   Why, doesn't Rover want it?

Wife   No. He had your steak and chips. I've just put him to bed with an Ovaltine-flavoured play bone.

Husband   Oh. Does this mean I'm kipping in the dog kennel again tonight, dear?

Wife   Well, yes. He's a thoroughbred, isn't he? He comes from a long line of champions – and you come from a long line at the Labour Exchange.

Husband   Do I? So that's why I'm so tired when I get home at night. Come, dear, let us get on with our illegal TV-watching.

THE DOOR IS OPENED BY SPIKE AND BLUTHAL. BOTH ARE

119

HOLDING WATER DIVINERS'
TWIGS.

Spike   This is the place.

Bluthal   Right, keep me covered.

SPIKE THROWS A BLANKET
OVER BLUTHAL. BLUTHAL
STARTS TO WALK TOWARDS THE
TV SET.

Spike   You're getting warmer.

Husband   Well, that's 'cos he's
near the fire.

SPIKE LOOKS SURPRISEDLY AT
HUSBAND.

Spike   We have a contact. Stand by
to materialise.

Bluthal   Wilko, Captain, you're
doing a great job.

Spike   No, I'm not. I'm standing by
the sofa.

SPIKE PULLS THE BLANKET OFF.

BLUTHAL IMMEDIATELY POINTS
AT THE HUSBAND.

Bluthal   Earthling, you have been
caught watching TV without a
licence.

WIFE TAKES HUSBAND'S
PROMPTING BOARD AND HE
THEN PUTS HIS HANDS UP.

Wife   It's true. We are a disgrace
to England. We have been watching
for seven years without a licence.

Spike   You have suffered enough.
We leave you now to think of a
funny pay-off.

SPIKE AND BLUTHAL EXIT.

Husband (*with hands in the air*)
Can you think of a funny pay-off,
dear?

Wife   No, they do have some
strange endings in this show. I
suppose we must be one of them.

The National Private Stylophone

A COUPLE ENTER A DOCTOR'S SURGERY. THEY ARE MIDDLE AGED – SPIKE PLAYS THE HUSBAND. HE WEARS A GROTTY MAC, MUFFLER, CAP. HE HAS A GREYING MOUSTACHE AND IRON-FRAME GLASSES. THE WIFE WEARS THE FEMALE EQUIVALENT OF HIS CLOTHES. THEY ARE LED IN BY A NURSE.

Nurse Mr and Mrs Arrgh.

DOCTOR IS VERY WELL DRESSED, PLAYS IT LIKE NOEL COWARD. COUPLE SIT BY DOCTOR'S DESK.

Doctor (*looks at them, tries several pairs of spectacles – shakes his head*) It's no good – they won't go away. Mr and Mrs Arrgh. How do you spell that?

Wife We don't.

VERY FIERCE LOOK BETWEEN DOCTOR AND WIFE. AS THEY LOOK AT EACH OTHER WE HEAR THE SOUND OF A VERY FIERCE CAT AND DOG FIGHT.

Doctor Do you want this privately or on the national health?

Wife National Health.

Doctor Now then, what appears to be the trouble?

Wife It's my husband.

Doctor Then you want a solicitor, not a doctor.

Wife No, my husband is ill, seriously. Suddenly, he cannot talk proper, like.

Doctor Has he ever talked proper, like?

Wife Not 'alf. 'E auditioned to take over from Angela Rippon. But he flunked it. Since then he's become difficult to live with.

Doctor Do you find him trying?

Wife Yer. Last night I found him trying with Mrs Soper on the back step.

Doctor That is not an illness.

Wife He soon had one, though. I fetched him one on the back of 'is nut with the coal shovel. Then I belted him on the back of his nut again, and I said, 'Bert, will you stop doing it while I try to talk to her.' It was that last blow that done something to his voice.

Doctor What?

Wife   You tell him, Bert.

SPIKE, BY USING A STYLOPHONE ON HIS KNEE UNDER THE TABLE, MIMES TO THE RHYTHM THAT HE TAPS OUT ON IT.

Doctor   Good heavens! The which of like I ever have I not seen which in my whole career, etc. Say the quick brown fox jumped over the lazy brown cow.

SPIKE MAKES APPROPRIATE NOISE ON STYLOPHONE.

Doctor   Amazing. Does he know 'Little Jack Horner'?

Wife   Well, if he lives in Deptford, yes.

Doctor   No, the nursery rhyme.

SPIKE TAPS OUT 'LITTLE JACK HORNER' ON STYLOPHONE.

Doctor (*to camera*)   Ladies and gentlemen, there is no known cure for this disease, therefore there is no known ending to this sketch.

LATE NIGHT WEATHER

Spike   Good evening. And now tonight's news of the weather. Well, it's been another burgly day in most areas, with slight multikertwigo in the North East. But mostly on the blans, blins and bluns. There'll be quite a bit of squirggling south of the brolls, but that should clear up by early wurslems. A ridge of high blundure is out here in the North Thunsplutzers and we might see some of that early tomorrow brunzling with a little throllicks on the squales. Otherwise, very snizzicks with plongs on the hillglund and low-glying wallingtons on the throcks. In other words, the sort of thing we can expect at this time of the year. So it's godd gluman fligwun from us.

Oh yes. Everton 1 and they deserved to.

The Welsh Miners

SPIKE AS WELSH MINER LYING IN BED (HE WEARS FULL RUGBY GEAR). OBVIOUS COAL MARKS ON FACE. THE WIFE (SHEILA STEAFEL) HAS AN OLD MANGLE AT ONE END OF TABLE, AND IDENTICAL COAL MARKS ON HER FACE. LINKS OF SAUSAGES COME THROUGH, AND OCCASIONALLY A SOCK APPEARS JOINED BETWEEN SAUSAGES. ALAN CLARE SITS AT THE TABLE AS THE SAUSAGES COME OUT. HE HITS THEM WITH A HAMMER. ALAN IS DRESSED LIKE A COAL MINER, IDENTICAL COAL MARKS ON FACE. HE MAKES GROWLING NOISES AS SAUSAGES GO PAST. ON THE KITCHEN RANGE A KETTLE IS STEAMING. ABOVE MANTELPIECE THERE ARE PICTURES OF LLOYD GEORGE, THE QUEEN, GANDHI AND DORIS DAY.

SPIKE HAS A BRASS BEDSTEAD WITH NO BOTTOM END.

THERE IS A CLOCKWORK CANARY IN A CAGE WHISTLING AWAY.

Spike   Oh dear, oh dear. Oh, lots of oh dear boyo. Here am I dying. Dying? It's better than working. Oh. hallo camera 3. If some viewers have just joined us, it only means that the programmes on the other networks are worse than ours.

CANARY STARTS TO WHISTLE.

Spike   Oh, the canary's whistling. That singing means that the air in here is still fit to breathe. It's amazing what airwick will do. We make him eat three every day.

Sheila (*very Jewish*)   My life, Gareth, ohh you don't eat, you don't eat enough to keep fit. My life!

Spike   How's that for monumental miscasting?

Sheila   How is your illness, Gareth?

Spike   The illness is fine, but I feel terrible.

Sheila   A nice bowl of soup I'll

make. Would you like a chicken or a tomato?

Spike   I feel like a leek.

Sheila   That's under the bed.

ENTER DOCTOR. HE CARRIES GLADSTONE BAG AND HAS IDENTICAL COAL MARKS ON CHEEK.

Doctor   Oh, good morning, Evans the bed. It's bad news, boyo. There's nothing more the national health service can do for you.

Spike   Would it make any difference if I saw you privately?

Doctor   Oh yes. I'd be twenty pounds better off. More hot water, Myra.

Sheila   It's coming, it's coming. What do you think? Hot water grows on trees?

Spike   Oh doctor, how much longer can you give me?

Doctor   Two days at the most.

Sheila   Oh, the place won't be the same without him – thank God!

Spike   Well, I can't grumble, I've had a good run.

Doctor   That's what's possibly made him so tired, then.

Spike   Look, doctor, I'd like a second opinion.

Doctor   All right, I'll give you one. It's the same as the first. That'll be another pound. I have carried out every possible medical test known to Llanelli Rugby Club and I'm afraid you must face up to the grim truth.

Spike   You mean?

Doctor   You mean what?

Spike   You mean swine.

Doctor   No, I don't mean swine – I mean (*turns to Spike*) brace yourself for this, boyo.

SPIKE PUTS BRACES ON.

Doctor   I mean he's fit to go back to work on Monday.

Spike   Next Monday. Good God. I was expecting at least another three months off to see me through the rugby season. Someone call the minister.

IMMEDIATELY THROUGH THE DOOR COMES A ROMAN CATHOLIC PRIEST RIDING AN ENORMOUS BICYCLE.

Priest   Morgan, boy, I've just heard the terrible news. Come, lad, let us pray to blessed Joe Gormley, patron saint of burning nuts.

SPIKE CROSSES HIMSELF.

Priest   Oh, you crossed yourself?

Spike   Why not? I've crossed everybody else. Now, dear Lord (*starts to sprinkle holy water over the bed*), Let us hope a miracle miners strike will help keep Evans the bed at home with his loved one, while the wife is out at work.

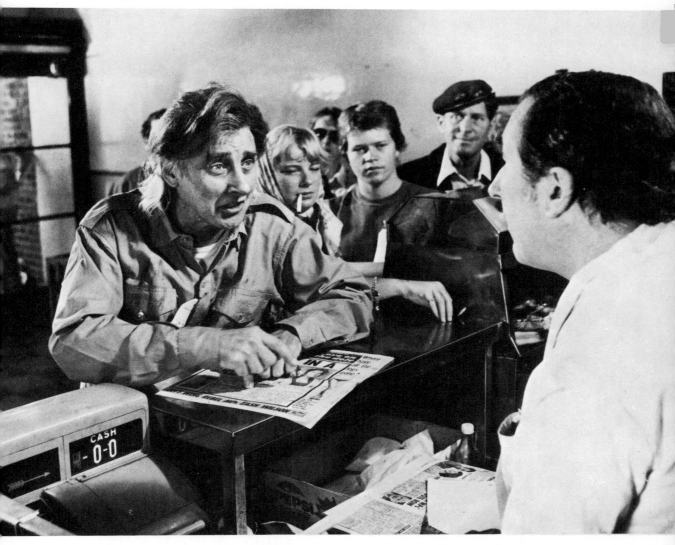

At the end of the series – Spike Milligan desperately seeking employment at the Finchley Labour Exchange as a floor sander. His mother lives in Woy Woy and is of little help.

THE PRIEST OPENS HIS BAG AND TAKES OUT A GIANT ROSARY. THE BEADS ARE LIKE IRON DUMB-BELLS WITH 56LBS WRITTEN ON EACH ONE.

Here, say this keep-fit rosary. If you're going to die you want to look at the funeral.

Spike Rosary? I thought you were a Welsh baptist.

BBC Studios burnt down by an angry audience at the end of the series.

Priest   No. Because 'tis well known in modern comedy sketches Welsh Baptists don't get half as many laughs as Irish Catholic priests.

Spike   Oh, I've got *news* for you, boyo. Come in, Evans the Prayer.

WE HEAR CRASHINGLY LOUD VERSION OF 'HALLELUJAH CHORUS' FROM 'THE MESSIAH'. ENTER WELSH BAPTIST MINISTER ON UNICYCLE. HE IS WEARING TOP HAT WITH SMOKE COMING OUT OF THE CROWN. A LOUD RED-AND-WHITE CHECK SUIT, CLOWN'S MAKE-UP BUT WITH VICAR'S COLLAR.

HE IS JUGGLING WITH THREE TENNIS BALLS. PHONE RINGS AND EVERYTHING STOPS.

Spike   Hallo what yes.

HE SMASHES PHONE DOWN
AGAIN.

Spike It's a miracle, I'm going
to be all right, boyo. That was the
colliery, I've been fired.

SPIKE GETS UP FROM BED,
GOES TO LITTLE COT BY
WINDOW. OUTSIDE WINDOW
THERE IS A BACKDROP WHICH
SHOWS GROTTY COAL MINE IN
VALLEY AT SUNSET.

THE SUN IS HAND OPERATED
AND IT GOES DOWN. FROM THE
COT, SPIKE TAKES A HUGE
BABY WHICH IS SIX FEET LONG
AND WHICH HAS BEEN
DOUBLED OVER AND WRAPPED
IN GIANT SHAWL.

Spike See that Cliff, little valley,
I mean that valley, little Cliff.
Either way it didn't get a laugh.
See that little labour exchange in the
valley, one day all that will be yours.

A SMALL TEAR APPEARS IN THE
BACKDROP. A FACE PEERS
THROUGH. IT HAS A TAM
O'SHANTER, RED HAIR, RED
BEARD, RED MOUSTACHE, RED
EYEBROWS.

Scot Can ye no keep bloddy quiet,
you Welsh creep, de ye no ken there
are Scots nationalists here trying to
sleep.

Voiceover Come in, comedy sketch
number four, your time is up.

SPIKE AND CAST EXIT
SLEEPWALKING.

Spike Milligan with his mother, who lives in Woy Woy and is of little help.